# FORAGING GUIDE

*Finding and Recognizing Local Wild Edible Plants and Mushrooms (2022 for Beginners)*

**Tiffany Snee**

# TABLE OF CONTENT

# INTRODUCTION

Bob was a straightforward individual. He went hiking one day and became disoriented in the mountains. He had gone early in the morning by himself.

For a brief moment, his thoughts had wandered. He was now lost in the forest, with no idea where he was.

To make matters worse, Bob had only brought a bottle of water with him that morning. He wasn't carrying a compass. He only had a small Army knife that he always carried with him.

Do you believe he will suffer from hunger? If you believe he will, you are mistaken.

Bob had mastered the skill of foraging. He knew which plants and mushrooms he could eat to keep himself hydrated while out in the wilderness.

He applied his knowledge and was able to survive despite the difficult circumstances. He might even say he had a good time in the mountain forest.

You don't want to learn about foraging when you're in a situation like Bob's.

The truth is that an increasing number of people are returning to the primitive ways of the hunter-gatherers' era. You can't hold it against them. If you knew the benefits of foraging, you would embrace the lifestyle as well.

Are you considering the benefits of foraging for food in the wild? The truth is that you are capable of accomplishing a great deal.

Foraging for food can help you live a healthier lifestyle. A diet of fresh raw food grown without the use of chemicals allows you to strengthen your immune system The food has not been processed in any way that is detrimental to your health.

When you go foraging, you can eat fruits, edible wild plants, fungi, nuts, and other things. This food can be consumed either raw or cooked. Many, if not all, of these meals contain more nutrients than the food we consume on a daily basis.

Foragers also discuss the medicinal benefits they derive from their foraging. This group of people uses a variety of medicinal plants in place of conventional drugs. One of the benefits of doing so is that, unlike traditional medicines, these plants do not have any side effects.

Do you want to get some exercise without going to the gym? It would be best if you considered a foraging lifestyle. The time you spend walking, bending, and searching for forage will help you get some exercise, which will make your body healthier.

You get the psychological benefit of feeling connected to the earth in addition to the physical benefits. Nature is an important part of our lives, and reconnecting with the universe will help you feel more at ease.

You are now aware of some of the advantages of becoming a forager.

Do you want to get started right away? Take your time!

One important thing to remember about foraging is that not all wild plants are edible. Some of these plants are extremely poisonous and can kill in seconds.

This fact does not have to discourage you. You can learn how to identify which plants and mushrooms are edible and which are not.

Do you want to know how you can learn this information? That is the goal of this book: to assist you in locating and identifying edible plants.

In your area, look for wild plants and mushrooms.

One of the most important things to remember when foraging is not to pick up plants you don't recognize. Most of the time, these plants will be harmful to your health. Even if they aren't, there's no way to tell because you don't recognize it.

As a result, it is best to avoid these plants.

You can still take this plant if you go foraging in a group and someone in your group recognizes it as edible. However, make certain that the individual is certain.

There is also an old adage that warns against leaving plants with three leaf clusters, such as poison ivy. Plants with milky sap can be hazardous to eat or even touch.

Before you go foraging, there is a lot you should know.

You do not, however, have to become overwhelmed.

This book will teach you everything you need to know about locating and identifying edible wild plants and mushrooms in your area.

It's time to say yes to a better life through foraging, and our guide will help you with everything foraging.


Have fun reading!

# CHAPTER 1

## *Forage*

### *What Exactly Is Foraging?*

The activity of gathering food from the natural environment is known as foraging. Foraging is the practice of gathering edible fruits, birds, insects, and animals from the wild. It also has something to do with catching birds and insects. Foragers also scavenge animals that have been killed by predators.

Foraging for food while hiking or mountaineering is a hobby for some people. They have provisions packed, but foraging rounds out the trip. Although, in some cases, it becomes a necessity rather than a hobby.

Humans have been doing this activity for a long time, aside from foraging for food while wildcrafting. It is one of the oldest methods of human survival for food.

Historically, some societies relied solely on foraging for food. The majority of these societies lived in desert and forest areas. Planting is not common in these locations because the plants would not grow.

In the past, some foragers also lived in fertile temperate zones. River valleys were present in some of these areas. These areas eventually became farmland.

The majority of people who live as scavengers have dogs. They do not cultivate crops or raise animals. Their dogs provide a significant portion of their income. They serve as foragers' pets, providing comfort and companionship. The dogs assist them in their hunting.

When scavengers are out scavenging, their dogs assist them in finding sources of food. Unfortunately, when there is no food or a famine, some scavengers will even eat their dogs.

Foragers are people who have been in the game for a long time. They assign roles because it is their primary source of income. The men would go on animal hunts. They would also scavenge the carcasses of animals killed by other predators. Plants were usually picked by the women.

Some activities can be performed by anyone, regardless of gender.

Gender lines blur in these situations. Anyone can do any aspect of the job. Activities such as firewood gathering can be done by anyone. Both men and women hunt for small animals and collect insects.

Some foraging societies are prone to rapid relocation. The availability of food in the area determines their settlement. As a result, they do not establish permanent living structures. Their movement is sometimes influenced by crop yield season.

Animals, like humans, forage. Human foraging, on the other hand, is more sophisticated and strategic. Humans are superior to animals and are enlightened. The knowledge of man has aided him in feeding and has resulted in better foraging methods.

Foraging has been practiced by humans since time immemorial. Foragers have always been the norm for humans. Humans have always relied on the earth for sustenance from generation to generation.

Humans have long relied on foraging as a means of survival. It is a practice that dates back approximately 200,000 years. Acquired knowledge and technological advancements have given birth to new ways of survival over time.

We now have supermarkets, shops, restaurants, and even online marketplaces. These changes have slowed the rate of foraging.

This is not to say that foraging is extinct. It is a practice that is still prevalent today. Foraging is popular among hikers, mountaineers, and tourists.

There are, however, various categories. These categories are explained further below.

### *Foraging Categories*

There are various types of foraging. People approach this exercise in various ways.

Some hunters concentrate their efforts on aquatic mammals and fish. This type of subsistence is known as aquatic foraging.

Equestrian foraging is the practice of hunting game animals with horses.

Some people forage for food on foot. Individual foragers and group foragers are two other types of foragers.

Some people forage on their own, while others forage in groups. Some foragers go mushroom hunting or gleaning.

## 1. Gathering

Gleaning is a type of foraging that uses farm leftovers. Farmers usually have leftovers when they harvest their crops for commercial purposes. Foragers collect plants for food.

Gleaning also occurs in harvested fields. Because there is no commercial gain in collecting these fields, they are left to grow.

Gleaning is considered a poor person's right in some parts of Europe, such as France and England. As a result, peasants were legally permitted to glean from farms and harvested fields.

England had a law in the 18th century that allowed people without lands to glean. It was their legal right to do so. These landless people were also known as cottagers. This constitutional right, however, expired in 1788.

The benefit of this type of foraging is that the likelihood of harvesting poisonous plants is low, if not non-existent. Farmers have ensured that the crops are edible because the plants were planned.

Foragers benefit from this method of foraging because they can be certain of the plants' freshness. Because the crops were grown by farmers, they are undoubtedly nutritious and fresh.

The benefit is bidirectional. Farmers benefit from this method as well. It is possible that some crops will be left behind after harvesting. Foragers harvest these crops to prevent them from going to waste.

## 2. Foraging for Mushrooms

Mushroom hunting is a highly specialized form of foraging. Foragers who follow this pattern are specifically interested in harvesting mushrooms for food. Some hikers and mountaineers only forage for mushrooms.

This type of foraging is also known as mushroom foraging or mushroom picking. It is a common practice in Korea, Europe, and Japan, among other places.

Mushroom foragers gather various edible mushroom species.

Mushroom hunting is a fun activity. Aside from being delicious, mushrooms have several other advantages.

Mushroom collecting requires extreme caution. There are poisonous species that are unfit for human consumption. If you are unsure whether something is edible or poisonous, avoid it entirely.

If eliminating mushrooms is a difficult decision, consult a guide. If mushrooming is on your list of wildcrafting activities, hire a tour guide. This e-book is an excellent resource.

## 3. Foraging in Groups

More than one person is involved in group foraging. Foraging can be done by families or groups of friends. A group of hikers or mountaineers may decide to go hunting as a group.

Foraging in groups is advantageous.

A number of hands are at work at the same time. A group of foragers can overcome obstacles more effectively than an individual. They can pool their resources and experiences to gather more food.

## 4. Foraging on One's Own

Individual foragers, as opposed to group foragers, gather food on their own.

He or she hunts for food on his or her own, without the assistance of a team. A hiker may choose to go foraging without the company of other hikers.

One advantage of this method is that the individual is able to keep the food to themselves. Whatever quantity is bagged is the individual's.

However, the number of foods gathered may be insignificant. In addition, the forager may require friends who have better results and can supplement his or her skills and level of expertise. It is not a bad idea if you choose to follow this pattern.

Because you are a one-person team, you should plan ahead of time how you will pack for your trip. Take the tools you'll need to help you exercise. If a problem arises, you should have enough information and tools to deal with it.

## 5. Foraging on Horseback

Equestrian foraging is a unique subsistence strategy. It is a dedicated gathering centered on a specific species.

Equestrian foragers use horses to hunt for animals. This type of foraging earned the moniker "equestrian," which is derived from the Latin word "Equus," which means "horse."

This type of forager can be found in Southern Argentina, North America, and even South America. This type of foraging thrives on horse breeding and horse riding ability.

There are numerous advantages to equestrian foraging. For one thing, it produces a large amount of output. Because the focus is on a single species, hunting them becomes more efficient. Foragers become experts at gathering these foods. Their catch is usually substantial. There are more food supplies.

This method of foraging is not without drawbacks. It does not allow for much diversity because it is a subsistence pattern focused on a limited range of species. The food collected and consumed is limited to the catch made.

Another disadvantage is that the food's consistency cannot be guaranteed. A natural disaster, such as an earthquake or a fire, can annihilate the animals that foragers hunt. Animals can be affected by an epidemic outbreak.

When such events occur and have an impact on the animals, foragers specialize in hunting. It may deprive them of food. It is a dangerous way to live.

## 6. Foraging in the Water

Aquatic foraging, like equestrian foraging, focuses on specific species. There are, however, distinctions between them. While riding a horse

Aquatic foragers catch marine animals and fish while terrestrial foragers catch large game animals.

The Latin word "aqua," which means "water," inspired the name of this foraging pattern. Aquatic foragers are common in the US, Canada, British Columbia, and other places. The Haida of Queen Charlotte Island forages extensively for aquatic foods.

Seaweeds, sea cucumbers, otters, crabs, sea lions, salmon, and other seafood are commonly foraged by aquatic foragers.

The benefit of this foraging system is its dependability. Foragers will always find food if they go foraging. Foragers along rivers and coasts have an advantage. Hikers and mountaineers are optimistic about catching fish.

## 7. Foraging on Foot

Foraging on foot is a common method of gathering food. This type of foraging is extremely mobile. Some foragers who engage in this pattern rely on it for a living.

They move around and live in temporary settlements. In seasons, they follow migrating herds and regionally available plants. The ! The Kalahari desert's Kung San or Zhu|asi are known for their pedestrian foraging.

Hikers and mountaineers frequently use this method. They can forage for food in fields around them while touring an area. Mountaineers can obtain food from the lands surrounding the mountains.

The benefits of this foraging pattern include a variety of harvests. There is the guarantee of a constant food supply. It is long-term sustainable.

## 15 Frequently Asked Foraging Questions

When embarking on a new path, it is normal to have some questions. Some questions will arise in the minds of anyone considering foraging. Some seasoned foragers may have one or two questions as well.

Here are 15 frequently asked foraging questions.

1. Why Should I Go Foraging?

This is an excellent question, but you should be able to ask and answer it yourself. Before you leave, make sure you have a good reason. It will keep you motivated when you face difficulties. It will also influence how you conduct your business.

People forage for a variety of reasons. Some foragers hope to foster a bond with nature. Some people seek food because they enjoy foraging for wild plants. You should understand why you forage.

2. What Are the Advantages of Foraging?

This is a common question among those considering foraging. Perhaps you know people who forage and want to join them, but you're not sure what you're getting yourself into.

Foraging is enjoyable, especially when done in a group. But, in addition to the enjoyment, there are obligations. Before you try it, you might want to know the advantages.

It is critical to understand the advantages of foraging because it will propel you forward. It will also give you a sense of accomplishment in the long run.

## 3. How Do I Get Ready to Go Foraging?

Before you pack your belongings and hit the road, you must thoroughly prepare. You must plan your backpacking trip carefully. You should consider the entire process, right down to foraging. It is a good idea to read foraging books and articles.

You may also make inquiries. If you know someone who has walked the path you intend to walk, take advantage of their wealth of knowledge. There are foraging guides for each category.

## 4. What Do I Need to Know About My Location?

You may do more than just climb mountains or hike if you are a hiker or mountaineer. You should go foraging. If this is your choice, make sure you understand the basics of the location.

Know your location well enough to avoid getting lost. Acquaint yourself with the terrain. Know your potential life threats and escape routes.

Make certain that you do not trespass. Use caution if you are not in a public place. Do not enter a private space. Know the laws that apply in your area and follow them.

You don't want your experience to be ruined. To be safe, consult a field guide. They most likely know something you don't.

## 5. When is the best time to forage?

After deciding on a location, you must do your research. Understand everything about it. But it doesn't stop there. You must be aware of the best time of year to visit there.

If this is your next step in getting ready to forage, you're on the right track. You can find a variety of things all year, but different plants have specific seasons.

Mushroom season lasts from July to mid-October. However, more mushroom varieties are available in September. April is a great month for a wide variety of plants.

6. What precautions should I take?

Everything revolves around safety. To have a pleasant backpacking and foraging experience, you must adhere to safety precautions. A location expert is useful in this situation.

If you have underlying health issues, address them before going wildcrafting. If you must travel, bring your necessities with you like drugs.

Take the proper foraging equipment. Keep in mind that not all wild plants are edible.

Go with a group if this is your first time. When you have gained some experience, you can venture out on your own.

7. Where Is the Best Place to Plant Forage?

Foraging is an enjoyable way to obtain edibles. However, you need to know where you can get enough fish to satisfy you.

The fundamentals are that you can forage wherever you go. You're likely to come across edible wild plants while hiking, mountaineering, or otherwise. These plants can be found in fields, forests, and other environments.

## 8. How Do I Make a Reservation with a Good Forage Company?

Your tour experience will be determined by where you book it. It is critical that you work with a reputable foraging company. Find good companies with a good reputation.

Request recommendations from friends and family members who have gone foraging in the past. Some tour companies are notorious for mishaps and poor customer service.

Before you make a deal with the company, learn about their policies and rules to see if they are suitable for you. Some businesses only hire during certain months. Some of these businesses are occasionally closed due to inclement weather.

## 9. What Equipment Do I Need to Forage?

The tools needed for foraging vary depending on the category of foraging.

The environment in which you will forage is also important. You might want to forage for food while hiking or mountain climbing.

Before you leave, you should decide whether or not you will forage and how you will do so. This choice will determine the tools to be used.

Another factor to consider is whether you will forage alone or in a group. If you go with a group, there is a chance that you will have all of the tools that are required If everyone pooled their resources, they could create useful hunting tools.

10. How Do I Identify Edible Plants to Forage?

While foraging is a great way to feed yourself and have fun, you must be cautious. Not all wild plants can be eaten. Some mushrooms are even poisonous.

It is a good idea to know what plants are commonly available in your area. You must also be familiar with the wild plants that are in season. Examine plants with white or discolored sap to see if they are edible. They are most likely not safe.

If you are unsure of the species of an edible plant, it is best to avoid it entirely. The general rule is to avoid eating anything that you are not certain is edible. Maintain your familiarity with any plant.

11. How Can I Avoid Dangerous Plants?

Make use of a field guide! Some edible plants resemble poisonous plants.

Some plants contain both edible and toxic parts. If in doubt, don't take the chance.

## 12. How Can I Gather Wild Plants and Mushrooms?

While foraging, you should know how to gather plants without killing them. It is best to use a knife or shears. Some plants should not be uprooted in order to preserve their species.

## 13. What Should I Do With My Harvest or Catch?

It is reasonable to inquire as to how you should handle your catch or harvest. It's one thing to forage; it's quite another to properly preserve your catch. The type of food you intend to purchase will determine how you will store it.

The most important thing is to understand how to transport and clean your harvest. You must also know how to skin your catch before eating it.

## 14. Is it legal to forage in the area I've chosen?

It is critical to understand the legal provisions in your area before going foraging. Legality differs between regions and even countries. In

Foraging could be considered theft in some places. In the United Kingdom, the 1968 Theft Act prohibits the sale of foraged produce.

If you're foraging in an uninhabited area, be mindful of private property.

If you must forage in a garden or farm, get permission from the owner first. Anything you take if you are not granted access will be considered theft.


15. Should I Join A Foraging Organization?

Foraging societies are made up of people who spend their entire lives foraging. They travel from location to location, gathering food and animals. It may be your desire to participate in these societies on occasion.

# CHAPTER 2

## *Mushrooms*

Mushrooms are a type of fungus that grows in the same way that plants do. They are frequently misidentified as vegetables. While this is not entirely incorrect, they are best described as fungus.

The button mushroom is the most commonly consumed species (Agaricus bisporus). It has historical significance because it was the first species cultivated in the Western world. It now accounts for more than 40% of global mushroom cultivation.

You might have wondered, "Who discovered these mushrooms?" at some point. You were probably blown away by their delectable taste in a soup. Perhaps you are captivated by their beauty. In any case, you most likely did not receive a response.

This chapter will teach you about the history of mushrooms.

The Evolution of Edible and Non-Edible Mushrooms

Mushrooms have undoubtedly been around for a long time. Over the course of their existence, man has extensively used them for a variety of purposes. The most common application is probably the production of delectable delicacies.

Mushrooms are described in a variety of ways, including delicious, lethal, and intoxicating. Some may even go so far as to include magical elements. Mushrooms have meant different things to different people throughout history.

Humans have long consumed mushrooms, according to food historians. Man has been eating these fungi, both edible and poisonous, since prehistoric times. Historians believe that man discovered it while hunting and foraging.

Without a doubt, our perception of them today is vastly different from that of the past. Hunters used to gather them and eat them.

It was a bit of a trial and error process. There were no happy endings in the majority of those cases.

Their cultivation method was unknown at the time. They could not be grown at home, unlike natural plants. As a result, they had to be gathered as needed. Many species are still unknown to be cultivated even today.

Some people dislike mushrooms because of the tragic outcome that resulted from their consumption. Even though some edible species are known, some people avoid them entirely. It resulted in the distinction of mycophiles and mycophobes.

People who enjoy eating mushrooms are known as mycophiles. Mycophobia, on the other hand, is the fear of mushrooms. People from the eastern hemisphere were predominantly Mycophiles. Mycophobes were mostly found in Western cultures.

According to a French philosopher, mushrooms changed Europe's fate. Many historians thought he was referring to the Austrian succession war. The war was said to have started after Holy Roman Emperor King Charles VI died.

Many people believe that the king died as a result of eating amanita mushrooms. Amanita, also known as death cap, is extremely lethal.

Poisonous mushrooms have killed several notable people. In 1701, the physicist who invented the Fahrenheit scale lost his parents to mushroom poisoning.

Johann Schobert, a French composer, died in 1767, along with his wife and daughter. This occurred after he insisted that a poisonous mushroom was edible.

They were welcomed on the other side of the world, however. They were consumed for their health benefits by the Chinese and Japanese, in particular.

These fungi plants had no names until recently in history. This was due to the fact that they were regarded as mysterious in many cultures. Mushrooms, for example, were thought to have immortality powers in ancient Egypt. As a result, only Pharaohs were permitted to consume them.

Similarly, it was only eaten by wealthy families in ancient Rome. Historians claim that Caesars used tasters to avoid poisoning. The tasters were to inspect the food to ensure it was safe to eat.

It was also said that the Greeks brought it from Libya. They were then sold along Europe's southern coast.

**Mushroom Discovery**

It's difficult to say who discovered mushrooms, where they were discovered, or when they were discovered. Archeological discoveries, on the other hand, show that mushrooms were used in prehistoric times.

There are rock paintings of mushrooms, for example, in Algeria's Tassili caves. These paintings are thought to have been around for around 7,000 years. Similarly, rock paintings dating back 6,000 years have been discovered in Spain. The evidence suggests that it was first used around 9000BC.

The Greek philosopher Hippocrates is credited with the first mention of them in Europe. Hippocrates is credited with the first documentation of their medicinal use. This Hippocratic document is thought to have been written around 400BC.

The word mushroom is derived from two French words. Fungi and mold are the two words. Even though this name is relatively new.

The Psilocybe mairei and Psilocybe Hispanics are prominently depicted in most rock paintings in Northern Africa. These two species are notable for their hallucinogenic properties.

Some experts believe that these species were used for medicinal purposes.

Documentation on its consumption in Egypt dates back to 4500BC. Mushrooms appear in many ancient wall paintings depicting plants. In addition, mushroom-shaped pillars were created. Many of which are still in existence today.

Many ancient Egyptian texts mention mushrooms, most notably 'the Egyptian Book of the Dead,' in which the author is quoted as saying, 'it's the food of the gods.'

In addition, an ancient poem attributed to Egypt says:

"Without leaves, buds, or flowers, they bear fruit; as food, tonic, or medicine: the entire creation is precious."

Mushrooms were used in rituals in ancient China, Greece, and Mexico. Even in Spain, some rock paintings depict the ritual uses of mushrooms.

There were many myths surrounding mushrooms at the time. Some speculated that it could unlock superhuman abilities. Others believed it could connect humans with the dead, while others believed it could guide one's soul. Some people believe it can also lead to the gods.

It may interest you to know that many of these beliefs persist to this day. Mexicans, for example, continue to use mushrooms laced with hallucinogenic substances in rituals. Participants in such ceremonies are said to see the gods.

Around the 1500s, the use of hallucinogenic mushrooms in Mesoamerica declined. Priestly writings from the 1500s extensively described the use and effects of the mushrooms.

Its use was quickly discouraged by Catholic missionaries. People were killed as a result of using the mushrooms in the area. It was only used in ritual ceremonies. Even so, most consumption took place privately.

These hallucinogenic mushrooms, also known as magic mushrooms, drew the attention of modern medicine in 1916. After reviewing some Spanish records, Dr. William Safford proved their demise. Nothing in the world, he claimed, could produce such intoxicating effects.

Throughout the 1930s, scientists flocked to Central America. Their mission was to determine whether such mushrooms existed or whether Safford's claims were true.

R. was not born until 1955. Gordon Wasson discovered the mushrooms. In Mexico, he took part in a ritual ceremony. Following that, he, along with his wife and daughter, participated in the rituals. In 1957, he wrote an article titled "Seeking the Magic Mushroom."

Albert Hoffman discovered that psilocybin and psilocin were to blame for the mushroom's hallucinogenic properties in 1962. After about 11 years of use, the drug was banned in the United States in 1968.

**Mushroom Cultivation in History**

There are some disagreements about how mushroom cultivation began. It is said to have started in 1650 in Western cultures. You may notice that the dates differ between texts. However, we know it started around the mid-1600s.

Contrary to popular belief, evidence suggests that mushroom cultivation began in China and Japan as early as 200 BC. Although it is speculative, some experts believe it could be older.

According to historians, Auricularia polytricha was the first species to be cultivated in ancient China. Auricularia polytricha is another name for ear fungus.

The mushroom was grown for its numerous medicinal properties.

Cultivation in Western culture began in France. The cultivation, which began by chance, is credited to a melon grower who lived in the Paris area. The species that was first cultivated was the button mushroom (Agaricus bisporus).

According to legend, the melon grower discovered the mushroom growing on manure. He decided to grow them commercially after making this discovery. Fortunately, his commercialization attempt was a huge success.

He sold them to restaurants throughout Paris after they were a success. Around this time, the mushroom earned the moniker "Parisian mushroom." This type of cultivation was practiced for a long time. This method is still used by some farmers today to cultivate Agaricus bisporus.

Years later, a gardener named Chambry in France discovered a better way to grow them. This fact, however, is not without controversy.

While some texts claim they are the same people, others claim they are two different people.

He discovered that mushrooms grow better in caves than in open fields. This benefit was provided by the caves' cold and moist environment.

This discovery altered the dynamics of French mushroom cultivation. People began to grow them in large quantities after that. Many caves in France are still used for this purpose today.

Mushrooms were not accepted in Europe until the 1800s, nearly 200 years later. It was initially accepted as a condiment in the United States. Mushrooms gradually became a part of Native American cuisine.

Many historians believe the French brought mushrooms to England and America. Within a short period.

It was well received by Americans. Foraging clubs sprouted up across the country. Their primary goal was to collect and identify edible species.

Farmers in America pioneered cultivation by using dark areas beneath greenhouse benches. A building was built in 1894 for the sole purpose of growing mushrooms. It was the world's first of its kind at the time. To this day, the structure is in Pennsylvania.

## Some Specific Species' Cultivation History

There have been numerous advancements in mushroom cultivation since its inception. Cultivation methods for various species are being developed on a daily basis. However, many of those inventions have recently emerged as a result of technological advancement.

However, our understanding of them is still limited in comparison to the number of edible species. Humans can currently cultivate only a few species.

Here are a few of those species and the methods used to cultivate them.

1. Mushroom Button (Agaricus bisporus)

This mushroom is well-known among many people. It is by far the most well-known.

It is the most cultivated species in the world, also known as the 'shop mushroom.' It was the only cultivated species in the world until the late 1970s.

The cultivation of this mushroom began in the 1600s. As previously stated, it began in France. For about 160 years, they were grown in open fields. It was later discovered that mushrooms grow from their spawn, or mycelium.

Growing plants from seeds were similar to this method. Later, it was discovered that light was not required for their growth in France as well.

This knowledge resulted in a shift from open field cultivation to cave cultivation. The French began growing this species in conventional houses in 1910. However, caves are still preferred for cultivation today.

Agaricus bisporus cultivation spread to England during the 1800s. It was introduced to the United States from England in 1856. Initially, mycelia had to be imported from England to the United States. These efforts were futile, as many of the spawns were damaged upon arrival in the United States.

There had to be indigenous spawns in the United States to compensate for this loss. One was successfully developed by scientists from the United States Department of Agriculture in 1903.

2. Fungus in the Ear (Auricularia polytricha and Auricularia auricula)

These two species are considered jelly fungi. They are the most widely consumed edibles in this category. Auricularia polytricha is mostly found in warmer tropical climates. Auricularia auricula, on the other hand, grows in temperate regions.

They may be the world's oldest known cultivated mushrooms. Their cultivation began around 200 years ago in China and Japan.

The species lives on its own. They feed on dead decaying things, as the name implies. As a result, they were grown on the trunks of dead trees in ancient China. It is still very much the norm today.

They are named after their distinctive ear shape.


3. Mushrooms, Oyster

This category includes mushrooms of the genus Pleurotus. Many of the mushrooms in this category have been cultivated over the years.

Prior to cultivation, they were primarily collected in North America and Europe. At the time, they were a popular species among foragers. They are still popular options today.

Nothing was known about their cultivation until the early twentieth century. A cultivation method for Pleurotus ostreatus was first described in the 1970s.


The species were grown on dead logs of wood using this method. The system was not particularly novel. It was more of a modification because it had been used in China for over 800 years prior.

The method was used by the ancient Chinese to grow other species. However, the technique was inefficient. The logs occasionally became infected and produced species that were not intended. This occurrence prompted several changes to the method to better suit its production.

4. Truffles (Tuber melanosporum)

Truffles are a specific type of mushroom. They are expensive and in high demand. A pound of Black Truffle (Tuber melanosporum) cost around $1,000 in 2011. In 2001, the white type (Tuber magnatum) was sold for between $1,000 and $2,200.

Despite the fact that the genus Tuber contains many species, only a few of them are edible. This species has been collected since 1600BC.

Many scientists developed theories about their nature and origins at the time.

Theophrastus is credited with being the first to propose a hypothesis about them. He described them as plants in his theory. He went on to say that their growth was caused by thunderstorms and rain.

This misunderstanding persisted for many years. Because truffles grow underground, this theory was accepted.

A plant pathologist from Germany proposed a different hypothesis in 1885. He elaborated on the true nature of truffles. He went on to explain that they had a symbiotic relationship with tree roots.

In the early twentieth century, his theories were rejected and then accepted. Even now, many people believe that truffles are the products of the trees where they are found. The complicated relationship between truffles and tree roots remains shrouded in mystery.

Many of the theories about the relationship that exists are mostly speculative. To this day, there are many unknowns surrounding its creation. There are no known cultivation methods as of yet.

Because of these mysteries, most truffle consumption has relied on natural collection. There was a drop in demand for truffles around the time of the world wars. This drop in demand resulted in a sharp drop in prices all over the world.

The once-valuable truffles have become obsolete. Farmers were forced to pull the trees where they grew. This was done to make way for more profitable crops.

The end of WWII saw a sudden increase in demand for truffles. Prices rose as a result of the scarcity of supplies. There was an urgent need to balance the growing demand for truffles with the dwindling supply.

Delmas and Grantee, two scientists, proposed a method of propagation in 1972. They proposed that trees be inoculated with Truffle mycelia.

The first trial was held in Europe five years later. A large area of land was used, which included Hazel and Oak plantations. After that, the trees were inoculated with Truffle mycelia. The first harvest took about ten years to complete, and it was a success.

The method was both efficient and long-lasting. As long as the trees were alive, they continued to produce truffles.


5. Morels Genus Morchella

Morel cultivation, like truffle cultivation, is poorly understood. They are expensive, just like truffles. However, unlike truffles, all morel species are edible.

Cultivating morels has been a problem for a long time. Morels were reported to have been cultivated in the fields in France in 1883. Molliard claimed in 1904 in response to the report. He claimed to have grown morels on compost made from apples. This claim was quickly debunked because the morels appeared to have grown naturally

Scientists have attempted to replicate them in rare environments where they are found. Unfortunately, the experiments were a failure because no morels were produced.

Morel mycelia were created in the 1950s. Mycelia were to be used as cooking flavors. This way of thinking quickly faded as people preferred morels to mycelia.

Ron Ower developed a propagation method in the United States in 1982. The technique was quickly abandoned because it was costly and produced few morels.

Ron and Gary Mills improved on the previous method three years later. Although it was superior to Ower's approach, the experiment was limited to Michigan. In terms of cultivation methods, there are numerous options available today. However, no one has succeeded in developing a profitable practice.

You are now aware that mushrooms have played an important role in many cultures throughout history. They were regarded as healthy food in Asia's eastern civilizations. They were fed to soldiers for strength in Rome. Many cultures considered them to be food for the gods.

Mushrooms separated the world into two groups: mycophiles and mycophobes. This disparity, however, is rapidly disappearing. Do you want to join the rapidly growing group of mycophiles who forage for mushrooms? The following chapter will teach you everything you need to know. Continue reading!

# CHAPTER 3

## *Foraging for Mushrooms*

When some people go hiking and see a mushroom in the forest, they simply turn around. When people who despise mushrooms see one growing on their lawn, they either kick it or chemically kill it.

It's understandable that these people dislike mushrooms because many are poisonous and only a few are edible. However, if you devote some time to learning how to identify edible mushrooms, you will be able to reap the benefits that mushrooms provide.

## Mushroom Identification

Some mushrooms are delicious to eat, while many others are toxic and cause severe or temporary discomfort. The majority of mushrooms are unpalatable or tasteless. The difficulty is determining how to identify the few edible mushrooms.

There are thousands of mushroom species worldwide, some with unusual shapes and others that do not resemble mushrooms. As you progress deeper into the mushroom kingdom, you will notice how complex and intricate the world of mushrooms is.

Identifying edible mushrooms, on the other hand, is not an impossible task.

There are procedures to follow, which are discussed further below.

**The Correct Method for Identifying Mushrooms**

Knowing the characteristics of various mushrooms is the first step in the mushroom identification process. This stage should be simple if your main goal is to identify a few mushrooms.

If you want to learn how to identify a wide range of mushrooms, you'll need a mushroom identification book. There are several mushrooms in the wild that resemble some edible mushrooms and can easily be misidentified as such. The mushroom identification book will help you distinguish between edible and lookalike mushrooms.

Apart from that, there are four stages to identifying any mushroom:

• Observation

If you know what to look for, any mushroom will gladly reveal its identity. What should you look for in a mushroom then?

Begin by inspecting its cap. Consider its length, width, color, and shape.

Check under the cap as well. Take note of its distinguishing characteristics, such as color, spacing, strip attachment, and so on.

The next step is to inspect the stem. Look for striations, stripes, rings, and other distinguishing characteristics.

Its substrate is also important to inspect. What and where is the mushroom growing?

Finally, confirm the growing season. Mushrooms grow at various times of the year. Check to see if it is growing at the appropriate time. If not, it's most likely a doppelganger.


• Examining

When you examine mushrooms, you smell, feel, and taste them. Edible mushrooms have pleasant aromas that can assist you in identifying them. If it doesn't smell good, it's probably not an edible mushroom.

It is also important to consider how the mushroom feels when touched. To the touch, edible mushrooms are usually smooth, fuzzy, slimy, and pleasant.

Finally, take a bite of the mushroom. Cut a piece of it and place it on your tongue before spitting it out. If it tastes bitter, it's a good idea to avoid it. And don't worry, spitting it out won't hurt you.

• Make use of Key

At this point, you pull out the mushroom identification book and examine the characteristics described in the book. If it's not what you think it is, it could be a different edible mushroom.

• Verify and Confirm Answers

Finally, if you've observed, examined, and cross-checked, it's time to make a decision based on the characteristics you've discovered. Keep in mind that if it does not agree with what the features say, stay away from such mushrooms.

## How to Spot Poisonous Mushrooms

There is no single rule that can be used to identify poisonous mushrooms. However, if you come across a mushroom, a few distinguishing characteristics can help you determine whether it's toxic or not.

Take note of the following guidelines to avoid picking poisonous mushrooms by accident:

- Avoid picking mushrooms with white gills.
- Avoid mushrooms that have a skirt or ring around the stalk.
- Red-capped or stalked mushrooms should be avoided.

These are not exhaustive because some edible mushrooms exhibit some of these characteristics as well. However, if you notice them, it's a good indication that you should avoid such mushrooms.

You may miss out on a tasty mushroom, but you can be certain that you will not become ill from eating a poisonous mushroom. It is important to note that you should not eat any mushroom unless you are certain it is edible.

**Mushroom Production**

You enjoy hiking and going for walks in the woods. But you don't want to go through the hassle of foraging for edible mushrooms every time you want to add some flavor to your meal. The solution is mushroom cultivation.

Mushroom cultivation is a sure way to get the type of mushrooms you require, whether on a small or commercial scale. Foraging for mushrooms is a gamble, especially if you are new to the game. Even experts make mistakes from time to time. But when it comes to growing mushrooms, you can't go wrong.

Also, those who prefer a specific type of mushroom may have difficulty finding it in the grocery store. In this case, growing your mushroom colony is the best solution for gaining quick access.

You can have more than enough mushrooms whenever you need them with just a few tools and the right growing system.

**Mushroom Cultivation Fundamentals**

Cultivated mushrooms are edible mushrooms grown on decaying organic matter.

To understand the essentials required for mushroom cultivation, you should be familiar with the classification of different mushroom species based on how they tap nutrients. The classifications are as follows:

**• Saprobic**

A Saprobic plant is one that grows on decomposing organic matter. Saprobic edibles are valuable as both food and medicine. They require a constant supply of organic matter to sustain their production in their cultivated form. Otherwise, it can be a production bottleneck.

**• Symbiotic**

A symbiotic mushroom grows alongside other organisms. They are mostly found on trees in the wild.

The mushroom assists the tree in gathering extensive water catchments and delivering nutrients from the soil that the tree cannot access.

**• Pathogenic or parasitic**

The majority of pathogenic fungi cause plant diseases. Only a few of these fungi are edible.The three major classifications of the thousands of mushroom species are as follows.

As a result, mushrooms are primarily cultivated in two ways:

1. Substrate Compiled

Organic materials derived from rice and wheat straw, hay, corn curb, composted manure, water hyacinth, and a variety of other agricultural byproducts such as banana leaves and coffee husks comprise composted substrates.

2. Substrate Made of Wood

Sawdust, wood logs, and other wood byproducts are commonly used in this method.

Six Crucial Steps in Mushroom Culture

The basic idea behind mushroom production or cultivation starts with mushroom spores. These spores develop into mycelium, accumulating massive amounts of stored energy and mass to support the final stage of the mushroom reproduction cycle.

The last stage of the mushroom reproduction cycle is the formation of mushroom or fruiting bodies. A complete cycle, from beginning to end, typically takes two to three months, depending on the mushroom species.

The following are the essential generic steps in the manufacturing process:

1. Cultivation Space Identification and Cleaning

You'll need to choose a room or structure to cultivate in and clean it. Choose a location where you can control the moisture, temperature, and sanitary conditions. These are the circumstances that govern spore growth.

2. Medium for Growth

As previously stated, there are two primary growing mediums for mushroom cultivation. Choose a growing medium that is easy to work with or that is appropriate for the growing environment you have chosen. The raw ingredients should then be stored in a clean area that is protected from rain.

3. Medium Pasteurization

Pasteurize or sterilize the medium, as well as the table or bags in which the mushrooms will grow. This sterilization prevents other fungi from growing on the same platform and competing for nutrients. When the mushroom grows, it colonizes the substance and fights off any competitors.

4. Seeding

After you've completed those steps, the next step is to seed the bed with spawn.

5. Coordination of the Growing Environment

This is the most difficult stage because the majority of the work is completed at this point. You must maintain optimal moisture, temperature, hygiene, and other conditions for mycelium growth and fruiting. You'll also need to add water to the substrate on a regular basis to keep it moist.

6. Recycling and harvesting

Harvesting is the final stage of mushroom reproduction. At this point, you can either eat your mushrooms or package them for sale. After that, you clean the room and begin again.


**Species Choice**

Most mushroom species only bear fruit in temperatures around 20 degrees Celsius. As a result, you're unlikely to find one growing in a temperate climate. To cultivate mushrooms, you should raise the temperature of the growing environment.

Aside from that, other factors to consider when selecting a species to grow include:

1. Waste materials are available for growing.

Not all mushrooms produce fruit in the same environment. Before selecting a mushroom species, you should first determine the type of substrate you have available.

2. Environmental Situation

Different species thrive in different environmental conditions. As previously stated, most mushroom species have difficulty growing in temperate climates. If you live in a tropical zone, you can only grow varieties that can withstand the conditions.

3. Your Field of Knowledge

Some species are difficult to grow due to the level of expertise required to produce them. If you don't know how to grow such species and don't have access to an expert, it's best to start with simpler species like oysters. Shiitake and maitake mushrooms are also good choices.

4. Your Available Resources

Aside from having enough waste materials to support the species you select, you must also consider the availability of the resources needed to grow such species.

Do you have what it takes to coordinate the environmental temperature in order for the species to survive? Consider other resources needed and decide if you want to try growing such species.

5. The market's demand

If you are only growing for personal consumption, you may not be concerned about the market demand. If you are growing for commercial purposes, however, you must consider market demand for such species.

Some people have an unrepentant bias toward one species while favoring another. To determine the best mushroom species to grow in your catchment area, you may need to conduct a market survey.

**Cultivation Methods and Key Species**

Here are some of the most commonly cultivated edible mushroom species that are widely accepted around the world.

**White Button Mushroom (Agaricus Bisporus)**

The white button mushroom is the most widely cultivated edible mushroom in the world, with the majority grown in temperate regions. The mushroom can be grown in a composted substrate.

When growing Agaricus Bisporus, you will need higher technology systems because a consistent temperature of 14 to 18 degrees Celsius is required. Though it can grow at higher temperatures, it must grow in a temperature-controlled environment to maximize its fruiting process.

**Oyster Mushroom (Pleurotus ostreatus)**

Oyster mushrooms are easier to grow than other mushroom species. As a result, they are the best option for beginning mushroom farmers. Furthermore, their farming process aids in the utilization of farm waste, making them an essential component of a sustainable agricultural system.

Oyster is typically grown on tree logs by cultivators. Recently, people began growing them on sawdust, rice or wheat straw, and other cellulose-rich waste materials. Oysters grown on high-cellulose waste materials have a fruiting period of about two months.

The substrate is placed in a plastic bag and kept cool and dark during the cultivation process. As the mycelium grows on the substrate, cut a hole in the bag to allow the fruiting bodies to develop.

**Shiitake Mushrooms (Lentinus edodes)**

Shiitake mushrooms are easy to grow and require few resources. Shiitake mushrooms can be grown both indoors and outdoors. Outdoors, it can be grown on a log, and indoors, it can be grown on sawdust or in bags.

The sawdust-based cultivation system accelerates the fruiting cycle and increases the yield. It does, however, necessitate more skilled management than when logs are used.

When you cultivate mushrooms with logs, the fruiting bodies appear faster as the diameter of the substrate logs increases. The durability of the product is also determined by the density of the wood.

**Paddy Straw Mushrooms (Volvariella volvacea)**

Paddy Straw Mushrooms are grown alongside rice crops. It can, however, be grown on substrates other than paddy straw, cotton waste, rice straw, oil palm bunch waste, and dried banana leaves. This method, however, produces lower returns.

Many mushroom cultivators in rural areas simply leave thoroughly moistened paddy straw under trees and wait for the mushrooms to grow.

**Mushroom Cultivation Requirements**

Mushroom cultivation necessitates a number of activities that can be performed by people with a wide range of interests, needs, and abilities. Find the essential tools for mushroom cultivation listed below.

1. Natural Resources

Land and climatic conditions play a minor role in mushroom cultivation, allowing farmers with limited land to participate. Furthermore, the unpredictability that plagues the traditional farming system does not apply to mushroom cultivation.

Access to sufficient and locally sourced spore substrate is a critical determinant of mushroom cultivation success. How easy and cheap is it to obtain agricultural byproducts, logs, or sawdust, as required by the mushroom species? Spores can also be obtained from mature fruiting bodies or purchased from local facilities.

## 2. Human Capital

Human assets are the skills, knowledge, and ability to work required to perform a specific job. Mushroom cultivation requires little human effort and can be used in conjunction with other tasks.

People with disabilities can also do mushroom farming and carry out the necessary tasks because it is not labor-intensive. Because the majority of the tasks involved are repetitive, people with mental disabilities can also grow mushrooms.

## 3. Physical Property

The physical equipment required to grow mushrooms is determined by the size of the production. However, many of the physical assets for mushroom cultivation are all-inclusive tools. These are common necessities such as water, transportation, energy, and buildings.

Mushrooms thrive in a cool, enclosed environment. You can easily maintain environmental elements such as temperature, humidity, moisture level, and proper ventilation in this structure. These conditions allow for proper development.

4. Financial Resources

The financial capacity required for mushroom cultivation is determined by the sale of the production. Because mushrooms can be grown on any scale, the financial investment required to start mushroom cultivation is minimal.

The system does not have to be massive. Furthermore, substrates in the form of agricultural byproducts or logs are frequently obtained for free.

In comparison to other agricultural and horticultural crops, mushroom cultivation systems allow for harvesting in a relatively short period of time. Mushrooms can be grown and harvested in two to four months. This is advantageous to small-scale producers.

**Mushroom Nutritional Values**

Though some mushrooms are poisonous, we cannot deny that they have nutritional and medicinal properties. While the nutritional and medicinal values of mushrooms vary depending on the species, some of the general benefits are listed below.

## 1. Nutritional Value

Mushrooms enhance the flavor of bland foods by adding flavor. They are also a valuable source of food in and of themselves. Fleshy mushrooms can be used in place of meat and contain enough nutrients to compete with a variety of vegetables.

Mushrooms can be added to a meal to provide a balanced diet, which is especially important for people in developing countries. They are high in vitamins B, C, and D, as well as minerals like copper, phosphorus, potassium, and iron.

They also provide carbohydrates while being low in cholesterol, fiber, and starch. They are also a good source of protein. Mushrooms have a higher protein content than kidney beans, ranging from 19 to 35%.

## 2. Medicinal Use

In addition to their nutritional value, mushrooms contain polysaccharides, which are beneficial to the immune system. Mushrooms are a perfect fit for the recently promoted functional foods and focus on other products "that are more than food."

Throughout history, mushrooms have been routinely added to Chinese traditional medicines. More than 6% of edible mushrooms are now used in many of today's health tonics and herbal formulas.

## Allergies and Intolerance to Mushrooms

Mushroom allergies mislead your immune system into thinking the proteins in mushrooms are dangerous. Histamine, the hormone that protects you from infections and diseases, is produced by the immune system. When this happens, your body reacts strangely, indicating that you are allergic to whatever you ingested.

Mushroom intolerance, on the other hand, is more genetic in nature. It has to do with your difficulty digesting mushrooms. As a result, you start having unpleasant physical reactions to them.

It is important to distinguish between mushroom allergy and mushroom intolerance. Mushroom allergy causes your immune system to react, whereas mushroom intolerance does not. Mushroom antigens can trigger your immune system even if you haven't eaten any mushrooms.

## Symptoms of a Mushroom Allergic Reaction

When you are allergic to mushrooms, you may experience gastrointestinal symptoms. The histamine released by your body causes inflammation and swelling of the intestine lining. Other mushroom allergy symptoms include:

- Nausea

- Light-headedness

- Diarrhea

- Headaches

- Hives

- Breathing difficulty

- Cramping

- Wheezing

- Bloating and abdominal pain

Mushroom allergies are a severe medical problem. If you experience these symptoms after eating mushrooms, you should consult a doctor.

**Remedy for Mushroom Intolerance**

Unfortunately, there is no preventative medication for mushroom intolerance. However, you can avoid eating mushrooms to avoid the unpleasant sensation caused by mushroom intolerance.

Because mushroom intolerance is caused by a problem with mushroom digestion rather than a problem with your immune system, this is the best possible treatment.

You now know everything there is to know about mushroom foraging. You can begin your search for edible mushrooms to include in your diet for their medicinal and nutritional value. In the following chapter, you will learn how to harvest and store mushrooms.

55

# CHAPTER 4:

## *Harvesting and Stockpiling Suggestions for Mushroom*

It is a rewarding experience to harvest your mushroom. However, because the process is time-consuming, it can be difficult.

The storing process can be even more difficult because it necessitates careful practice. It may take some time to learn how to do it correctly, but as you practice, you will gain a better understanding of the process.

To begin, only bright, unblemished mushrooms are harvested. It's best if you only use mushrooms that look and smell fresh.

Avoid mushrooms with bad spots that are dry, darkened, shriveled, moldy, and have an unpleasant odor. Such mushrooms cannot be stored for an extended period of time.

**When to Pick Mushrooms**

Mushrooms are not like other plants in that they have a predictable growth period. The general rule is to wait patiently for the mushroom to emerge from the compost. The time it takes to grow is determined by the type of compost you use, as discussed in the previous chapter.

It also depends on the type of mushroom you choose to grow to some extent. However, the mushroom should appear in three to four weeks on average. Wait until the caps open, when they change from convex to concave, to harvest them.

The size of the mushrooms does not indicate when they should be harvested. Bigger does not always mean better. You can, however, choose to wait until they are large enough if you prefer.

**Mushroom Harvesting Methods: Cutting or Picking**

Harvesting mushrooms is not a big deal, nor is the process mysterious.

However, there is some debate about whether it is better to pick or cut the mushroom. The debate over which technique is best will not go away anytime soon, as each method has its supporters.

Those in favor of cutting the mushrooms argue that doing so will destroy the surrounding mycelium, which has yet to develop or is still developing. They also claim that the method increased yield over time.

Those who favor picking argue that cutting can leave stumps where diseases can develop and contaminate the growing medium.

Which technique should you use after considering both sides of the argument? The answer is straightforward because, in reality, there is no distinction between the two methods.

They both have drawbacks that, if handled properly, will be irrelevant in the end. As a result, your goal as a mushroom forager is to master whichever technique you choose to employ.

**Mushroom Picking and Cutting**

If you choose to cut mushrooms, use a sharp knife placed at the mushroom's stem. Also, remember to remove any remaining substrate material and cut in such a way that the stem does not protrude out of the growing system.

If you want to pick the mushroom, gently pull it out of the substrate with your fingers. Separate them carefully from the substrate so that your mushrooms look beautiful from the bottom of the stem to the top of the cap.

The objective is to pick the mushrooms with care. The key to success is to be gentle!

Remember that the mycelium must remain active and alive for continuous growth and harvesting in both methods.

## How to Keep Mushrooms

Mushrooms do not last long before deteriorating. They can be useful for up to a week after harvesting if properly stored.

If you want to keep them that long, put unwashed mushrooms in a brown paper bag, fold the bag from the top, and store it in a cool, dry place.

However, if you need them to last longer than a week or if you want to sell them for a profit, you must use mushroom preservation methods.

There are two main methods for preserving mushrooms: refrigerating or freezing and drying.

## Freezing or Refrigerating

To extend their shelf life, store them at temperatures ranging from 2 to 4 degrees Celsius. Fresh mushrooms do not freeze well, and freezing them will not keep them from decomposing.

If you only need to keep fresh mushrooms for a short time, wrap them in paper bags and place them in the freezer.

Otherwise, cook the mushrooms before freezing them. Cooking destroys the enzymes that hasten the deterioration of mushrooms. As a result, this step is critical, and there are two ways to complete it.

## 1.  Sautéing

Sautéing food means cooking it in a small amount of fat, usually oil, in an open pan.

Wash and slice the mushrooms in cold water. (No soaking) Depending on the number of mushrooms, sauté for about 5 minutes in butter or oil. Freeze the mushrooms on a cookie sheet for a few minutes. When they are partially frozen, transfer them to a freezer-safe container and store them there.

**2. Steamed**

Freezing alters the color and texture of the mushrooms, turning them dark and soft. Follow these steps to reduce the color change.

- Add one teaspoon of lemon juice or citric acid to one pint of water.
- Soak the mushrooms for about 5 minutes in the mixture.
- Then, depending on the number of mushrooms, steam for about 5 minutes.
- On a cookie sheet, flash-freeze Place in a freezer bag or containers.

**Mushroom Drying**

Drying your mushrooms is a simple way to keep them fresh for a long time.

You can dry your mushrooms using a variety of methods. Among the methods are using a food dehydrator, a kitchen oven, a box fan, sun drying, and so on.

Whatever method you choose, the general drying process includes the following steps:

- Cut the mushrooms into bite-sized pieces. It speeds up the drying process.
- Avoid overheating them because heat can destroy some of the mushrooms' beneficial components.
- Check on them on a regular basis to prevent over-drying. The goal is to extract all of the water from the mushrooms. As a result, they must be cracked dry in order to break apart or snap easily.
- After drying, store in an airtight container in a cool, dark place.
- If you are allergic to mushrooms, use caution when drying them. While drying, heat and air movement can cause spores to move around.

These are the steps to drying your mushrooms. Adjust them to your preferred drying method.

Keep in mind that too much moisture on your mushrooms can make drying time-consuming. As a result, avoid washing the mushrooms before drying them.

Now that you've learned everything there is to know about mushroom foraging, harvesting, and storing, you might be wondering if there are any other plants you can eat in your area. The following chapter will teach you about wild plants, how to find and recognize them, and how to harvest and store them.

# CHAPTER 5

## *Wild plants*

Plants that grow on their own are known as wild plants. People frequently regard them as a nuisance to other plants. Smaller ones are frequently considered weeds and removed from the midst of plants.

These plants are referred to as "wild" because they frequently grow in places where they are not wanted. They grow on their own, without the intervention of humans.

There are, however, edible and medicinal wild plants. Some are aromatic and perfumery in nature.

The advantages of wild plants are numerous and varied. Farmers can earn a lot of money from these plants. Foragers also take advantage of nature's gift by gathering wild plants. Some edible wild plants are edible raw. Some necessitate cooking or drying.

However, not all wild plants are edible. Some are poisonous and should be avoided at all costs.

Wild plants grow in a variety of habitats. They are abundant in fields, coastal areas, and other places. You can find out more about where to see wild plants.

**Where Can I Find Wild Plants?**

Wild plants do not have a limited growing area. They will grow anywhere if not planted. These plants do not require human care to grow and produce.

Gardeners will never be able to eliminate them from their flowerbeds. Even when they die, these plants regenerate or are replaced by new ones. As a result, the battle against weed is ongoing.

Weeds, like other plants, grow in farms. There are stages in crop farming where farmers weed because they are unwanted.

Wild plants thrive in open spaces and wild places such as fields, wastelands, wetlands, mountains, and hills. They can also be found in uninhabited areas and along the coast.

They grow without being cut in these areas. Because they grow to full size, these plants provide a pleasing sight in these areas. You might wonder if wild plants are useful for more than just a beautiful view.

Hikers and mountaineers, on the other hand, forage for wild plants. Some people enjoy foraging as a hobby. However, it is a survival strategy in some places. Wild plants can be extremely useful if used correctly.

## Wild Plant Applications

Because wild plants grow almost entirely on their own, one might conclude that they are not as useful as other plants. This assumption, however, is incorrect. All over the world, wild plants are beneficial. They play critical economic roles in rural areas.

• Financial Gains:

Any society's economy benefits from the use of wild plants. This is especially true in developing countries. Wild plants are essential wherever agricultural practices exist.

Local communities with thriving agricultural systems rely heavily on wild plants. It is a source of nutritious food. Foragers in these areas include tourists, hikers, and mountaineers.

Wild plants provide a variety of foods. Plants' roots, stems, leaves, fruits, seeds, tubers, and other parts are edible.

Most wild plants are eaten raw in some places, such as Turkey. They consume raw Rumex alpinus and Rumex chalepensis stalks. However, some plants must be boiled or dried before consumption.

Some wild plants are used in the production of food additives and processing agents. Bee plants aid in the production of honey. Wild plants are also used in the production of wine and beverages.

Some people cook with wood fuel. They take them from the forest and cut them up into usable pieces. Some people prefer to purchase from those who cut them. These plants typically provide financial benefits to farmers. These products' consumers provide a ready market for producers and sellers.

• Socioeconomic Gain

Wild plants have socioeconomic value as well. They can be processed and used to make dyes, fibers, and building materials. Parts of wild plants are also used to make resins, tannins, latex, oils, and wax.

Plant parts are also used as constituents in cosmetics and perfumes. Such plants include Achillea spp., Rosemarinus Officinalis, and others.

Wild plants are also used to make medicines for both humans and animals. These medications are used to prevent and treat diseases and illnesses.

The significance of medicinal plants cannot be overstated. These plants are typically grown close to the home in most communities. Aloe inermis, Aloe perryi, Salvia fruticosa, and other medicinal plants have been used for thousands of years. Medicinal plants continue to play important roles in drug production today. Recent research has even revealed the importance of these plants.

The majority of countries, particularly developing countries, base their healthcare systems on traditional medicines. According to the World Health Organization (WHO), the figure is 80 percent.

Fuelwood, charcoal, and fertilizer are also made from wild plants.

The value of wild plants is regarded as central to some traditional knowledge. Some wild plants are used by indigenous communities. Most of the time, culture is preserved and passed down.

Wild plants are vital to nature in general. They are vital to the survival of some birds and insects. Some of these insects may become extinct if these wild plants are no longer available for them to feed on.

Insects are drawn to the presence of these wild plants. Farmers can use it as a natural pest control method. These insects will not infest the plants that surround these wild plants. The insect will instead feed on wild plants.

Farmers should consider allowing wild plants to grow near their crops. However, weeds can be removed from among the plants.

**A breathtaking view of nature**

Another fantastic benefit of wild plants is the view they provide. Nature affects human minds. A pleasant view of the natural environment is good for one's health.

Despite the benefits of wild plants, some people cut them off. Some farmers and gardens cut them off right away. Everyone will benefit if wild plants are preserved.

**The Environmental Importance of Wild Plants**

Wild plants play an important role in restoring the natural environment. Aside from being attractive, they also help to improve the soil. They also function as windbreaks. It makes them extremely valuable in high-wind areas.

Wild plants can also aid in erosion control. They are also used as decorations.

Most people do not fully utilize the benefits of wild plants because they perceive them to be harmful. The general public is not well informed about the benefits of having wild plants around.

You should no longer be a part of this crowd now that you know how to use these wild plants. You can begin foraging for these plants using the guide provided in the following chapter for locating and identifying these plants.

# CHAPTER 6

## *Fifty Edible Plants in North America*

In North America, you can forage for a variety of edible plants. However, the majority of these plants are regarded as weeds. If you look closely around you, you'll notice several of these edible plants sprouting nearby.

Don't pass up these nutrient-dense plants the next time you're out foraging. This list will assist you in identifying what is edible and distinguishing it from poisonous varieties.

### Chickweed

This is an annual herb that grows on lawns in the spring. It doesn't like the heat, so you'll find it in the shade. It thrives in moist soil.

leaves of these plants fold up when it is about to rain, which is a distinctive feature.

## Identification

It has five small white-colored incised flower petals that appear to be ten. Only one side of the slender stem is hairy.

After each leave pair will appear on a different side.

The leaves are oval in shape with pointed tips. It lacks a milky sap, unlike other plants.

When the stem is opened up, it has an elastic pith that does not crease when the outer stem is bent.

The leaves grow in opposite pairs, which switch directions at each node. Older plants frequently have and can grow to be 12 inches (30 cm) tall.

## Edible parts

The flowers, stem, seeds and leaves of chickweed are all edible.

## Safe Consumable Quality

Consume only a small amount. Too much of it can cause stomach upset.


## Best Consumable Condition

Chickweeds can be eaten raw or cooked as part of a stew or soup.


## Nutritional    value

Chickweeds contain a lot of minerals and vitamins. It's high in vitamin C, potassium, calcium, selenium, magnesium, beta-carotene, and other nutrients.


## Location

It grows in open fields and on lawns.

**Fireweed**

This lovely plant could be mistaken for another flower brightening the field where it grows. It is, however, an edible plant that can be eaten in the wild if you are in need of food.

The plant is known as the Rosebay Willow Herb or the Great Willow Herb in the United Kingdom.

**Identification**

It has a simple, smooth reddish stem with lance-shaped leaves that alternate in a scattered pattern. The flower of the fireweed is large and pinkish, with four petals and stigmas. The plants grow very tall, with dwarf species reaching heights of 12 to 14 inches (20-60cm).

It has a vein structure with a circular pattern. This feature distinguishes it from other toxic lily plants in early spring when they tend to look alike.

**Edible parts**

In early spring, you can eat the flower, leaves, and stem. They have a bitter taste and are tougher in the summer.

Because the pith of older plants can be eaten raw, you can extract it by splitting the stem open.

The roots can also be eaten after roasting and scraping off the outer layer, but they have a bitter taste.

**Safe Consumable Quality**

You are free to eat as much as you want.

**Best Consumable Condition**

When the leaves of fireweed are ready to eat, you can eat them raw or cooked. The shoots can be pickled or sautéed.

**Nutritional    value**

It contains a lot of vitamins A and C.

**Location**

Fireweeds can be found on stream banks, open woods, hillsides, arctic seashores, open fields and pastures, and alpine slopes.

**Wood Sorrels**

These plants come in a variety of colors and frequently bloom in the spring and fall. It has a mild lemony flavor that will keep you hydrated when you're out in the wilderness.

## Identification

The plant's leaves are compound, with three heart-shaped leaflets folded along the mid-vein. They can be purple or burgundy in color, but the majority are green. These leaves fold up at night and open up in the morning, and they may also fold up in direct sunlight.

Its five-petaled flowers can be white or yellowish. At the same time, some other varieties' petals may be violet or pinkish in color.

Its seedpods extend about 90 degrees from the stalk on which it grows. Stalks grow at roughly the same angle as the main stem.

## Edible parts

All parts of this plant are edible. Its edible parts include the leaves, seeds pods resembling tiny okra fruits, flowers, and roots.

**Safe Consumable Quality**

Consume in moderation because the high oxalic content can be toxic.


**Best Consumable Condition**

Wood sorrel can be eaten raw or as a seasoning in food. It could also be used as a coffee flavoring or as part of a salad dressing.


**Nutritional     value**

The vitamin C content of Wood Sorrel is high. Some species are tuber plants that are high in fiber, amino acids, and proteins.


**Location**


Wood sorrel can be found in the woods and on forest floors.

**Mustard Greens**

If you come across this invasive weed anywhere near you, it's time to go get some for your belly. Its garlic-like flavor makes it an excellent addition to your meals.


**Identification**

Depending on how close the leaves carve in at the midvein, the leaves of these plants are kidney-shaped or heart-shaped. Its edges break off in a sharp, irregular pattern, though younger leaves may appear scalloped. This plant's leaves may or may not be hairy.

There are five white petals, six stamens, and four green sepals on the flower.

Four of the stamens are usually tall, while the other two are short.

Typically, the flowers bloom between May and June.

**Edible parts**

Mustard green seeds, roots, stems, flowers, and leaves are all edible.

**Safe Consumable Quality**

Because of the cyanide content, eat the leaves in moderation or soak them in water before eating.

**Best Consumable Condition**

Garlic mustard leaves are best eaten in cool weather because they become bitter in hot weather. However, regardless of the season, the leaves are edible.

You can use the flowers in salads and save the seeds for later in the season. The spicy roots can also be harvested at the start of spring or at the end of fall. When the plant has yet to flower, you could also add the stem to your vegetables.

**Nutritional value**

Green mustards are high in vitamins A, E, and C, as well as beta-carotene. It is also high in fiber and contains manganese, calcium, iron, and zinc.

**Location**

Garlic Mustard grows in swamps, ditches, disturbed forest floors, roadsides, and along fence lines. It is widespread in many parts of the United States and Canada.

**Wild Black Cherries**

These attractive fruits are full of flavor and make a tasty snack for those who are fortunate enough to come across some. When it fully matures in early fall, its reddish or blackish-purple drupe will be appealing.

## Identification

The leaves of these plants fall off in an ovate pattern, lining the branches of the trees alternately. It is typically 6 inches long.

The bark of the tree is smooth and light brown, but it may become darker and rougher with age. The branches are long and slender, and they can grow to touch the ground.

The flower cluster can be found at the plant's branch tips. Close inspection reveals that the white flowers have five petals, five sepals, and several stamens. They bloom on a raceme that is about 4-6 inches long.

After the flower bloom, the fruits appear at the end of the raceme, initially green, then dark red, and finally purplish-black at full maturity.

## Edible parts

Although the fruits are edible, they may taste bitter.

## Safe Consumable Quality

Because of the cyanide content of its seed, this fruit should only be consumed in moderation.

## Best Consumable Condition

It can be eaten raw or pressed to extract the juice.

## Nutritional    value

Wild black cherries are a good source of vitamin C and antioxidants for the body.

## Location

Various species can be found in many parts of Canada and the United States. You might come across one in a park, field, or open forest.

# Alfalfa

Alfalfa is one herb that can be found in the wild if you are looking for wild herbs for food. It is highly regarded for its medicinal properties and is grown by some people. You might be lucky enough to find it growing on its own somewhere near you.

## Identification

This plant prefers moist to wet soil and does not grow in a shed. It can reach a height of 1m, and it blooms from June to July, with seeds maturing from July to September.

The leaves of the Alfalfa plant are divided into three narrow leaflets with serrated edges. The middle leaflet sticks out more than the others.

Purple flowers appear in clusters on a raceme and can have 10 to 30 flowers per cluster.

Its seed pods spiral and can contain up to six seeds per pod.

**Edible parts**

Alfafa leaves, seeds, and shoots can all be eaten.

**Safe Consumable Quality**

Even if you find this plant in abundance, it is best to eat only a small amount of it. It has the potential to endanger red blood cells.

**Best Consumable Condition**

The leaves are edible both raw and cooked. You may want to boil it for a long time to reduce the saponin content. Salads could benefit from the sprouted seeds.

**Nutritional    value**

Protein, vitamins A, B, C, and K are abundant in the plant (the leaves)

**Location**

It's most common in meadows, woodlands, disturbed fields, and riverbanks.

**Dandelions**

This plant's beautiful flowers make it easy to identify among other weeds.

## Identification

Dandelions grow as close to the ground as possible. The leaves emerge at about 90 degrees from the stem rather than upwards as in some closely related species.

The leaves have smooth, sharp tooth-like edges. They have no hair on their surface and their stems may produce milky sap. The stems are usually whitish but can be purplish.

As with any sunflower species, the flowers are bright yellow. However, identifying dandelions by their flowers may be difficult because many other varieties share the same flower structure.

## Edible parts

Both the leaves and the roots are edible.

## Safe Consumable Quality

Consume dandelions in moderation. You should also avoid it if you are pregnant or nursing.

**Best Consumable Condition**

To preserve its nutrient base, it is best eaten raw or lightly cooked. It could also be dried and powdered and used to season food.

**Nutritional      value**

It's high in vitamin K, beta-carotene, calcium, and omega-3 fatty acids, among other nutrients.

**Location**

It is found in grassy areas and disturbed areas.

**The Curly Dock**

Finding a tender curly dock plant while foraging can be worth the effort. When you come across the tender one, you'll discover a rich green vegetable that tastes like spinach.

**Identification**

As the name implies, the leaves of this plant are long, narrow, and curly. They grow close to the ground as well as high on the stem. The leaves at the base, on the other hand, are longer and wider than those on the stem.

A whitish sheath may be found around the nodes, which will eventually turn brown with age.

The flowers, which are often purplish, can grow in clusters of up to 25. They are typically small and insignificant.

The seeds are enclosed in a leaf-like capsule that grows on the stalk. They are frequently three-sided, with one side pointing sharply outwards. The case of the seeds may turn brown with age, but it often remains on the stalk throughout the winter.


**Edible parts**

The leaves, stem, seeds, and roots of the curly dock are all edible.

For a rich flavor, harvest the stem before it flowers. For the best flavor, collect the freshly unfurled leaves. The seeds and roots can also be processed and harvested.

**Safe Consumable Quality**

To avoid consuming too much oxalic acid, eat curly docks in moderation

**Best Consumable Condition**

Depending on the season of harvest or the part of the plant you're eating, you can eat it raw or cooked.

**Nutritional    value**

It is high in vitamins B, A, and C, as well as iron.

**Location**

This plant can be found near roadsides, construction sites, and disturbed fields.

# Chicory

This plant is a common weed that you've probably seen growing in a variety of places, particularly along roadsides. When in full bloom, its beautiful edible flowers can be quite enticing.

## Identification

The harsh, hairy stem often produces pointed leaves. They are lance-shaped and grow in alternate patterns. The leaves are frequently broader at the base and have lobed edges.

The flowers are sky blue, pink, or white in color and only open when it's sunny. They have a parallel shape and overlap each other.

The stem contains a milky sap, and the leaves become thinner as they grow upward. The plant has a system of tap roots.

## Edible parts

All parts of this plant are edible. The stem, leaves, flowers, and roots are all edible.

## Safe Consumable Quality

Chicory roots and leaves can be consumed in any amount. If you eat it raw, you may have to deal with its bitter taste depending on how much you eat. However, it is not considered safe for pregnant women.

## Best Consumable Condition

This plant can be eaten raw, but it is best boiled to remove the bitter taste.

**Nutritional value**

It is high in fiber and contains B vitamins.

**Location**

It is a widespread weed in North America. It grows in old fields, along roadsides, and in weedy areas.

**Creep Charlie**

You might be lucky enough to come across this nutritious green while hiking in the woods.

**Identification**

The leaves are round or kidney-shaped with scalloped edges and grow on long stalks. They grow in pairs on the stems and are greener than the plant near the top of the stem. The surface of the leaves is sparsely hairy.

The stem of the plant is square, and the root is fibrous. The stems carrying the flower are more upright and have smaller leaves.

If a node on the stem touches the floor, the plant will usually form a mat and can form another root. When the plant has finished flowering, it grows quickly.

The flowers are typically blue to purplish in color and have two-lipped petals in a tube-like shape. The flowers are arranged in groups of three.

## Edible parts

This plant's young leaves are edible and will add a minty flavor to your meals.

## Safe Consumable Quality

You are not at risk as long as you consume Creeping Charlie in moderation.

## Best Consumable Condition

This plant can be eaten raw, but it is best boiled to remove the bitter taste.

## Nutritional    value

It is high in fiber and contains B vitamins.

## Location

It is a widespread weed in North America. It grows in old fields, along roadsides, and in weedy areas.

## Harebell

It is also known as bluebells or a lady's thimble. It does not appear to be edible, but it can be a good source of food. If you come across this plant while foraging, don't be afraid to pick some for food.

## Identification

The leaves of this plant are frequently kidney-shaped and can grow to be up to 7cm long when mature. The leaves at the plant's base are frequently round. Those at the stem's tip are usually thinner and grass-like.

The plant's sap is milky and flows when the leaves or stems are broken. Because of its lightweight, the stem is narrow and may even hang downwards.

Its flowers are bell-shaped, which is probably why it is called bluebells. Purple flowers appear on the thicker stalk with narrow leaves. On the outside, they have five spoon-shaped lobes.

From June to September, the flower is in bloom.

**Edible parts**

This plant's leaves are edible.

**Best Consumable Condition**

You can eat the leaves raw in salads or cooked with your meals.

**Nutritional    value**

This plant is well-known for its high levels of vitamin C.

**Location**

Harebells can be found in wooded areas, meadows, beaches, and both shaded and open areas. They are common in most of the United States and Canada.

**Broadleaf Plantain**

This is yet another unusual edible weed. On the surface, it may appear frightening, but if you ever find it, you will have free food.

**Identification**

It is distinguished by its large, oval-shaped leaves and thick stems. The stems emerge from a base. The flowers are greenish, long, and have erect spikes that grow from the bottom leaves.

The flowers are composed of four petals, a pistil, and two stamens. The seeds develop beneath the flowers.

**Edible parts**

Broadleaf plantain leaves and seeds are edible and have numerous medicinal applications.

**Safe Consumable Quantity**

Don't overeat the seeds because they can cause bloating.

**Best Consumable Condition**

The leaves can be eaten either cooked or raw. It has a bitter taste, and harvesting the seeds can be difficult.

**Nutritional    value**

These plants contain tannins, flavonoids, and glycosides, all of which are anti-inflammatory compounds that can aid in inflammation reduction.

**Location**

Broadleaf plantain can be found on playgrounds, walkways, and open fields.

**Pineapple Weed**

It is an annual plant that is frequently confused with chamomile. When crushed, it emits a pineapple-like odor.

**Identification**

It is a low-growing plant with finely divided foliage that, when crushed, emits a pineapple scent. Pineapple weed has a greenish-yellow flower head that is cone-shaped.

The leaves are divided into fine, feathery segments. They can grow to be 2 to 4cm in length and are hairless.

The entire plant can reach a height of 30cm.

**Edible parts**

Both the flower and the leaves are edible.

**Safe Consumable Quantity**

Every night, drink a cup of pineapple weed tea.

**Best Consumable Condition**

The flowers can be dried and crushed to make flour. Tea can be made from the leaves.

**Nutritional    value**

This plant can be used to treat fever, stomach upset, and insomnia. It also has analgesic properties and is especially beneficial to breastfeeding mothers.

**Location**

This plant grows in the cracks of sidewalks and almost all waste areas, and it can even survive in abused soil like driveways, dirt roads, and sandy soil. It is widespread in North America.

## Mallow

You can identify a Mallow plant if you are familiar with the hibiscus flower or the hollyhock. The only distinction is its broad leaves.

### Identification

The leaves are distinct and round. The flowers and seed pods are small and round and are frequently obscured by the leaves. Mallow possesses a funnel shaped flower with five petals and a distinct stamen column surrounding the pistil.

The fruits are round and have wedges that look like cheese. The stems are flexible and grow from a single point on the ground.

The stem grows from a deep taproot and is low spreading, with branches up to 60cm long.

Flowers are produced singly or in clusters from the axils.

## Edible parts

Edible parts include the leaves, stems, flowers, seeds, and roots.

## Safe Consumable Quantity

It's best to limit your consumption to a reasonable amount.

## Best Consumable Condition

It can be eaten raw or cooked, just like vegetables.

## Nutritional    value

Mallow contains calcium, magnesium, and iron.

**Location**

This plant can be found in most parts of North America. This plant thrives in lawns, gardens, roadside ditches, and waste areas.

**Coneflower**

This fast-growing plant produces seeds and is simple to cultivate. To match your garden, you can find them in bright, purple, or subdued colors.

**Identification**

Coneflowers are easy to recognize. The flower has a rounded shape and stands upright. The lower leaves are larger than the upper leaves. The stem is stiff and covered in thin, vertical purple lines. The stems can branch into lateral limbs or they can remain straight and unbranched.

The lance-shaped leaves emerge alternately and singly from the stem. They have cone-shaped centers with seeds that attract butterflies. Coneflowers are drought tolerant and easy to grow.

## Edible parts

Coneflowers are edible in all parts, but the leaves and flower buds are used to make herbal tea.

## Safe Consumable Quantity

You are free to take as much as you want.

## Best Consumable Condition

Herbal tea is made by drying the flower and leaves.

## Nutritional    value

It boosts the immune system, lowers blood sugar levels, alleviates anxiety, and cures colds and skin cancer.

## Location

It's common throughout most of North America.

**Elderberry**

The European elder tree produces this dark purple berry. It is frequently confused with American Elder, Dwarf Elder, and Elderflower, but they are not the same thing.

**Identification**

Look for small white flower clusters, drooping purple fruit, and hard, woody bark. Elderberry typically grows in a bushy, shrub-like form. Mature elderberry plants can grow to be 9 to 12 feet (2.7 to 3.7m) tall.

Elderberry thrives in moist environments.

**Edible parts**

These plants' fruits, flowers, and petals are edible. Safe Consumable Quantity

You can eat as many fruits as you want. When made into tea, however, it should not be consumed more than three times per day.

**Best Consumable Condition**

Raw fruits and petals are consumed. The flower can be fried after being dipped in batter.

**Nutritional    value**

It contains a lot of vitamin C and fiber.

**Location**

Elderberries can be found on stream banks, marshes, and moist forests.

**Meadowsweet**

This plant is the most beautiful and fragrant of all hedgerow plants. It has creamy yellow flowers and scents the neighborhood with honey, vanilla, and almonds.

## Identification

The tree can reach a height of one or two meters. The dark green leaves have up to 5 pairs of toothed leaflets surrounded by smaller leaves. The top surface is smooth, while the undersides are slightly hairy. When the flower first opens, it emits a pleasant scent. When the flowers fade, the smell intensifies.

The fragrance of the stems and leaves is not as strong as that of the flowers.

## Edible parts

It has edible leaves, blossoms, buds, and seeds.

## Safe Consumable Quantity

It is safe in small doses, but a high dose can act as an anticoagulant, preventing blood clotting.

## Best Consumable Condition

The leaves are edible both raw and cooked as a green.

## \Nutritional    value

It contains a lot of carbohydrates, sugars, and vitamin C.

## Location

It is found throughout most of North America.

## Pepper Grass

This mustard family plant has a spicy flavor. It goes well with salads, soups, pasta, and other dishes.

## Identification

The raceme on this plant grows from the plant's highly branched stem. Flowers bloom at the racemes' tips.

This plant produces tiny white flowers with four petals, two to four stamens, and a length of 1 to 3mm. It has four cupped, greenish-white sepals that are approximately 1mm long.

The leaves are hairy and lance-shaped. The leaves are basal at the plant's base and can grow to be 2 to 15cm long, with a large terminal lobe and a variety of lateral lobes.

**Edible parts**

The entire plant can be eaten.

**Safe Consumable Quantity**

Consume as you see fit.

**Best Consumable Condition**

To make tea, combine the leaves with salad or grind the roots.

**Nutritional    value**

It is high in protein, iron, and vitamins A and C.

## Location

The plants are widespread in North America. The plant grows along roadsides, disturbed areas, pastures, and waste areas.

## Field Pennycress

Stinkweed, Frenchweed, and Fanweed are all names for field pennycress. It can grow as a winter or summer annual plant.

## Identification

The seeds are oval in shape and dark brown in color. They're rounded on one end and taper to a point on the other.

The stems are winged along the ribs and ribbed. The alternate leaves can grow to be up to 4 inches long and 1 inch wide. The leaf margins are wavy and sometimes have sharp teeth.

The root system is similar to that of a taproot. The flowers are small, measuring about 18 inches across when fully opened, and have four white petals and four green sepals.

**Edible parts**

Both the seeds and the leaves are edible.

**Safe Consumable Quantity**

A decrease in white blood cells may result from high doses. It is not safe to use during pregnancy or while breastfeeding.

**Best Consumable Condition**

The leaves can be eaten either raw or cooked.

**Nutritional    value**

It's high in protein, fat, carbs, and oil.

## Location

Nursery plots, areas along railroads and roadsides, fallow fields, gardens, and cropland are all common places to find Field Pennycress.


## Purple Deadnettle

This plant is also known as the "devouring purple monster," a name given to it to describe its effect during the winter season, when its purple color can turn an entire field purple.

**Identification**

It is a seasonal plant. The hairy nettle does not sting, thus the name "dead nettle," and it is commonly found near wastelands and sidewalks.

The leaves are triangular in shape, and the stalk connects to the stem blade. The flowers are pink and have a tube-like shape. The lower and upper ends are angled inward.

The stems are square in shape, with a greenish color at the bottom and purple shades at the top

**Edible parts**

The only edible part of the plant is the deadnettle leaves.

**Best Consumable Condition**

The leaves are edible and can be used in salads, smoothies, soups, and tea. As a result, you have the option of eating it raw or cooked.

## Maximum Consumable Quantity

Consume the leaves in moderation.

## Nutritional    value

It has medicinal properties. It is anti-inflammatory, anti-fungal, and anti-bacterial in nature.

## Location

Purple deadnettle can be found in most gardens across North America.

## Forget me not

This flower is thought to represent true love. Flowers are used to decorate gifts in the hope that the recipients will remember who gave them. During the evening, the flowers emit a lovely fragrance.

**Identification**

The flowers have greyish-blue petals that range in size from 3 to 5mm. The curved flowering stalks open to reveal a slew of five-lobed flowers.

The leaves and stems are hairy and soft. Upper leaves do not have stalks and alternate along the stem. The plant's branch can grow to be 40cm tall.

The fruits are 1.5 to 2mm long and mericarp egg-shaped. They are glossy, with narrow wings that are yellowish-brown in color.

The plant can be found on roadside medians, woodland edges, crumbling walls, and hedgerows.

**Edible parts**

This plant's flowers are edible.

**Safe Consumable Quantity**

The flowers are non-toxic and can be consumed as often as desired.

**Best Consumable Condition**

The flowers can be eaten raw as a snack, tossed in a salad, or used to garnish desserts and meals.

**Nutritional    value**

The entire plant is used as medicine to treat nosebleeds and lung problems.

**Location**

The plant is widespread in North America, with some species indigenous to California.

**Mullein**

This plant is distinguished by its soft leaves and yellow flowers at the top, which gives it a distinct appearance.

## Identification

This soft biennial plant grows to be quite tall. During its first year of growth, it produces rosette-shaped leaves.

The tall stem, which resembles a pole, bears a dense spike of yellow flowers. It spreads its seeds, but it is not aggressively invasive. Its seeds germinate in the open.

Flowers range in size from 5 to 60cm in length and have five petals, hairy green sepals, stamens, and one pistil. Each flower is replaced by a seed capsule, which contains two cells and numerous tiny seeds.

A basal rosette is formed by large oval-shaped leaves. It has gray-green leaves that can grow up to 50cm in length.

## Edible parts

The leaves and flowers are edible.

## Safe Consumable Quantity

You can consume this weed as often as you like.

## Best Consumable Condition

The leaves and flowers are edible as a salad and can be boiled to make tea.

## Nutritional value

It is high in antioxidants and is used to treat the common cold and asthma. It is also beneficial for muscle relaxation.

## Location

It is widespread in the United States and southern Canada. Mullein can be found in open fields, railway embankments, disturbed areas, and landfills.

## Thistle (Bull Thistle)

The top of this plant is covered in short, sharp prickles, and the leaf blade is dark green. The prickles make it difficult to touch the surface.

## Identification

Purple flower heads measure 3.5 to 5cm in diameter and 2.5 to 5cm in length. The bracts on the flowers are narrow and spine-tipped.

The leaves are lance-shaped and alternate. On top and underneath, they have rough, bristly hairs. The leaves range in length from 7.5 to 30cm.

The stem is thorny and firm. It produces many seeds with small feathers that are attached to the base by a ring until they ripen. It prefers to grow and survive in disturbed environments with moderate moisture.

## Edible parts

The root, flower stems, leaves, flower buds, and seeds are edible.

**Safe Consumable Quantity**

Consume as you see fit. However, avoid its thorny parts.

**Best Consumable Condition**

Other vegetables can be combined with the root. The flower stems and young leaves can be cooked and eaten in salads. It is possible to prepare the flower buds and roast the seeds.

**Nutritional value**

It contains a lot of inulin and protein. It can also help with liver problems and type II diabetes.

**Location**

Bull thistle is widespread and can be found throughout North America.

**Kudzu**

This vine is well-known for its rapid and erratic growth. It is a highly invasive species with a daily growth rate of up to 30cm.

**Identification**

Each node has three leaflets that form the leaves. The stalk connects the leaves to the stem. The central leaf's petiole is about 19mm long, and the other two have shorter petioles.

Small, brownish bristles on the long vines trail on the ground or climb vertical surfaces. They are capable of covering an entire tree or entire building structures. The woody vines are thick.

The flowers are purple or reddish-purple and are arranged in clusters. The flowers can reach a height of 8 inches.

**Edible parts**

The vine tips, leaves, flowers, and roots are all edible.

## Safe Consumable Quantity

To determine if you are allergic to it, a small portion should be eaten the first time. If not, you are free to consume as much as you want.

## Best Consumable Condition

The leaves can be consumed raw, chopped, baked, or fried. The root is frequently used to make tea.

## Nutritional value

It contains a lot of calories, protein, carbohydrates, fiber, and fat.

## Location

It's native to the southeastern United States.

## Pickerelweed

The leaves and flowers of this aquatic plant are above water, while the stem is underwater.

**Identification**

This plant can be found in shallow waters. The flower stem rises above the leaves, with only one leaf growing behind the flowers, and it has one spike of small flowers and heart-shaped leaves.

The flowers bloom one after the other, from the bottom to the top.

This method of flowering extends the flowering period by several days.

The flowers can reach a height of 6 inches.

Fish, birds, reptiles, and swimming mammals use the large leaves as a home.

Its dense root system acts as a wave barrier, preventing shoreline sediment erosion. The leaves are 10 to 25cm long and have long petioles.

**Edible parts**

The seeds and leaves are both edible.

**Safe Consumable Quantity**

You can eat as many nuts as you want, but make sure the water source from which you harvested the weed is not polluted.

**Best Consumable Condition**

The seeds are edible as nuts, and the leaf stalks can be cooked as greens.

**Nutritional value**

It contains a lot of vitamins and minerals.

**Location**

This plant can be found throughout most of North America.

**The Red Clover**

The red clover is an edible plant in the legume family. Its origins can be traced back to the Chinese, who used it medicinally. It was also thought to be a powerful cure for burns and bronchial problems by Native Americans and other notable cultures.

## Identification

The reddish flower of red clover gives it a distinct appearance. Its head is composed of various tubular-shaped flowers. It has green leaves with pale green or white chevrons on the plant's upper side. This characteristic protects the plant from pollinator insects.

The leaves are oval and broader in the center of the plant. Each compound leaf has two stipules at the base.

## Edible parts

Red clover has the best flavor of all the clovers. The red clover flower is the most edible part of the plant. The leaves can also be consumed in salads or tea.

## Safe Consumable Quantity

To avoid side effects such as nausea, rash, or headache, eat it in moderation.

## Best Consumable Condition

It is not recommended to overeat the flower because it may cause bloating.

## Nutritional value

It is high in vitamin C and contains minerals such as potassium, phosphorus, calcium, and magnesium.

## Location

It is found throughout most of North America. They are commonly found in pastures and fields and can grow to be about 80 centimeters long.

**Partridgeberry**

Partridgeberry is a member of the madder family, with stems up to 20 centimeters long. It's distinguished by a pair of white tubular flowers with red berries. They are also known as twinberry.

**Identification**

Plant stems range in color from light green to light brown. They eventually turn brown and smooth as they age. The flowers are radially symmetrical and measure approximately 13-16 mm in length.

The flowers are found at the axils of the leaves or at the tips of the branches. Each pair of flowers has the same tubular calyx.

Partridgeberry leaves are oval in shape with smooth margins. It has a shiny upper surface and a dark green color.

**Edible parts**

The plant's berries and leaves are both edible, but the leaves are usually used to make tea. The fruit has a neutral flavor and can be used in any recipe.

**Safe Consumable Quantity**

It is relatively safe to consume, but pregnant women and breastfeeding mothers should avoid it.

**Best Consumable Condition**

The dried leaves can be used to make tea, and the berry flesh can be eaten.

**Nutritional value**

It contains a lot of protein, fiber, and calories.

**Location**

They are typically found in rocky uplands, sandy savannas, and wooded ravine slopes. It is especially common in eastern North America.

**Sorrel Sheep**

Sheep Sorrel is one of North America's most common edible wild plants. It's a perennial plant in the Buckwheat family. It spreads its horizontal roots and produces seeds to grow. They stand between 10 and 40 cm tall on average.

**Identification**

It is easily distinguished by its arrow-shaped leaves, which grow in a rosette. Underground, a creeping root system connects the growing leaves. The sheep sorrel and dock seed are both members of the same species, as evidenced by their seed heads.

Because of their creeping root, they typically grow in patches. The flowers are unisexual, with male varieties being yellowish in color. Females, on the other hand, are reddish-green in color. They are small, with whorls and a branching cluster.

Unlike common sorrel, which has a pointed leaf base, the bottom of the leaves are lobed out. The middle leaves are short-stalked and have lateral lobes on both sides.

**Edible parts**

The leaves can be eaten. Foragers typically use it to thicken soups or grind it into flour to make noodles. It has a lemon or tart flavor and tastes like citrus or apple peel.

**Safe Consumable Quantity**

It is best consumed in moderation. Overeating can cause nausea.

**Best Consumable Condition**

The leaves can be consumed raw or cooked.

**Nutritional value**

Vitamin C is abundant in the plant.

**Location**

It is common in North American forest areas.

## The Shepherd's Purse

The shepherds' purse usually appears in the early spring. As the plant begins to flower, the basal leaves wither, leaving only the smaller leaves.

## Identification

Their purse-shaped seedpods help to identify them. It is a member of the mustard family and can be distinguished from others by its lobed basal leaves. The leaves can grow to be about 10 cm long.

The first set of leaves is usually rounded, while the later set is deeply toothed. Shepherd's purse frequently grows to 30cm is the average height.

## Edible parts

In salads, it can be used in place of cabbage or cress. Both the seeds and the flowering shoots of the shepherd purse are edible parts of the wild plant. Ginger can be substituted for consumption by drying the root.

The leaves are generally available all year and can be dried for later use.

## Safe Consumable Quantity

Consume in moderation, and pregnant women should avoid it.

## Best Consumable Condition

The leaves can be eaten raw or cooked, depending on your preference.

## Nutritional value

It contains a lot of iron, vitamin C, and calories.

## Location

Most of North America is familiar with the plant. They are commonly found in grain fields, along roadsides, in waste areas, and in gardens.

## Sunflower

Wild sunflowers have a showy ray petal that attracts butterflies and birds. They are the non-cultivated version of the sunflower.

The main source of nutrition for the sunflower is photosynthesis, which is why the sunflower and its leaves turn to follow the sun - they are phototropic.

## Identification

They are annual plants that have hairy, coarse, and leafy characteristics. They typically reach a height of 1.5 meters and have a stiff and upright stalk. Their yellow florets will draw your attention immediately.

The top of the flower has a reddish-brown central disc. The flowers are surrounded by 40 to 80 ray florets.

Their leaves have a scratchy and rough texture and can grow up to 30cm in length. The upper part of the leaves are covered in short, stiff hairs. Their petioles are light green to reddish in color and covered in short, stiff hairs. Sunflowers do best in areas with alkaline soil.

**Edible parts**

It can also be ground into a powder and mixed with flour to make bread. The leaves petioles are edible when boiled with other vegetables.

**Safe Consumable Quantity**

Consume as many seeds as you like.

**Best Consumable Condition**

The seeds can be eaten either raw or cooked.

**Nutritional value**

They contain a lot of protein, Vitamin E, and magnesium.


**Location**

They are commonly found in landfills, fences, roads, and fields.


**Spring Beauty**

Spring beauty, or Claytonia carolianais, grows from a starchy rhizome. The rhizome stores energy from previous seasons to propel its growth early in the spring.

The yellow circle and pink veins on the flowers serve as pollinators for this wild plant.


**Identification**

The Montiaceae family includes the spring beauty. It is a type of perennial species that blooms in the spring. It can be identified by its pink or white petal with dark veins.

The ripening of the seed capsules usually results in the plant disappearing above ground.

Each flower has six white petals surrounded by pink veins. A pair of leaves grows on the stems, and each leaf is about 8cm long and 2cm wide.

**Edible parts**

The roots, leaves, and stems can all be eaten. Their roots are starch-rich and have a nutty flavor.

**Safe Consumable Quantity**

Eat as much as you want.

**Best Consumable Condition**

Raw or cooked, the roots, leaves, and stems are edible.

**Nutritional value**

It contains a lot of vitamins A and C.

**Location**

They typically inhabit forests, open woods, wetlands, and alluvial thickets.

**Tea Tree**

Camellia Sinensis is another name for the tea plant. It is the source of various teas such as white, yellow, black, and oolong tea.

The leaf buds and leaves are used to make tea. What distinguishes one tea color from another is the method of production used by the producer.

## Identification

It is classified as an evergreen shrub, but if left alone, it can grow into a tree. It has a lifespan of up to 50 years. Their flowers are always white and fragrant. They occasionally appear in groups of two to four.

Plant flowers are hermaphrodites, and bees pollinate them. The leaves are dark green in color and have a pointed tip. The leaves are hairy on the underside and can grow to be about 8 cm long. They are commonly found at forest edges in shaded areas with high elevation. It grows best in areas with sandy or partially loamy soil.

## Edible parts

The leaves can be eaten or used to make tea. If you want to fully benefit from the leaf's nutrients, eat it raw. Consumption of tea flowers is also permitted.

**Safe Consumable Quantity**

Consume it in moderation.

**Best Consumable Condition**

Tea leaves can be eaten or used to make tea.

**Nutritional value**

Flavonoids, amino acids, and proteins are found in tea plants.

**Location**

It is found in the warmer parts of North America.

**Toothwort**

The Brassicaceae family includes the toothwort, also known as Dentaria diphylla.

**Identification**

It blooms in the spring and remains a woodland groundcover throughout the summer. After flowering, the plant goes dormant and returns in the fall. Flowers on the plants bloom from March to April.

Each flower has four petals that range in color from white to pinkish. Toothwort has basal leaves with a long petiole. In general, the wild plant can reach a height of 30 to 40 cm.

**Edible parts**

Leaves can be added to salads or sliced into soups. The plant's root has a strong flavor, especially when first harvested. If the root is fermented for three days, it will develop a sweet flavor.

**Safe Consumable Quantity**

Consume it in moderation.

**Best Consumable Condition**

The plants' leaves and roots can both be eaten raw or cooked.

**Location**

North America is home to the toothwort plant. They are typically found in the northeastern United States, Ontario, and all the way down to the Maritimes in Canada. The plant is mostly found in moist woods and meadows.

**Teasel**

Dipsacus fullonum is another name for teasel. It is a biennial plant that is easily recognized. The plant is self-fertile and has been observed to attract wildlife. The plant produces rosette leaves in its first year and grows to about 2.5 meters the following year.

## Identification

Teasel is distinguished by its thick taproot and fibrous secondary roots. The flower forms a ring in the middle of its head after the first year. It then grows for a few days before withering, leaving behind two rings that grow in opposite directions.

The entire flower head is about 50 to 100 cm tall, with a single flower measuring about 12 mm.

The flowers are lilac in color and bloom between June and September on the plant. Flowering stems are usually upright and branch near the top of the plant.

## Edible parts

Both the leaves and the roots are edible.

## Safe Consumable Quantity

Consume as you see fit.

## Best Consumable Condition

The leaves can be eaten raw, cooked, or blended into a smoothie. The roots can be made into vinegar or tea.

**Nutritional value**

It contains a lot of fiber, vitamin C, and flavonoids.

**Location**

Teasels can be found in sunny areas all over the world. It can be found on the sides of roads, in pastures, in abandoned fields, and in wastelands.

# Wild Grape Vines

Vitis Riparia, or wild grapes, are deciduous vines with a voracious growth pattern. Its growth can cast shade on nearby trees or bushes.

This plant grows in dozens of locations around the world. They are perennial plants that outgrow most native vines.

## Identification

Grapevines typically produce deep-lobed leaves that resemble cultivated grapes. Because of its forking tendrils, it climbs very well during its growth. They are typically purple, black, or dark blue in color. The plant produces tiny flowers measuring about 10 cm in length.

The flowers bloom in early summer, before the green grapes appear. The leaves alternate along the stem and can reach a length of about 15 cm. They have an orbicular shape and are either faintly or deeply lobed.

The edges are toothed and have a hairy texture. Wild grapes can reach a height of about 17 meters.

**Edible parts**

Wild grape tastes better after the first frost, but ripe grapes can also be eaten. When you turn the grape into juice, you will thoroughly enjoy it.

**Safe Consumable Quantity**

Consume it in moderation. It could quickly add up in terms of carbs and calories in your body.

**Best Consumable Condition**

The leaves can also be eaten raw or in salads. The fruit is also edible raw.

**Nutritional value**

They are high in vitamin A, vitamin C, carbohydrates, and protein.

**Location**

This plant has up to 60 species in North America.

**Wild Bee Balm**

Wild bergamot is another name for wild bee balm. It's a fragrant plant that draws bees, birds, and butterflies. Native Americans commonly use it to treat common colds.

Creeping rhizomes give rise to wild bee balm.

## Identification

The rough lavender or pink color of wild bee plants distinguishes them from other plants. The plant is drought resistant and thrives only in sunny, dry conditions. Monarda didyma is similar to the wild bee plant but can be distinguished by its bright red color.

The flowers are fragrant, and they bloom from the center of the flower head outward. It blooms for about a month, beginning in May.The alternate leaves are ovate or lanceolate in shape and color.

The environment will determine whether the leaves turn light or dark green. In their lifetime, wild bee balm can reach heights of 30 to 70 cm.

## Edible Parts

They are typically used to season cooked foods or salads. The flower of wild bee balm can also be used to garnish salads.

**Safe Consumable Quantity**

It is acceptable to consume it in moderation, but pregnant women should avoid it.

**Best Consumable Condition**

The leaves are edible both raw and cooked.

**Nutritional value**

Caffeic acid is present.

**Location**

The plants are typically found along the edges of limestone glades, fields, and thickets.

**Mallow Vervain**

Vervain mallow was once thought to be a cultivated plant, but it now thrives in the wild. It's a natural source of green, yellow, and cream dyes.

They thrive in areas with a balanced pH or are alkaline-rich.

**Identification**

Its delicate flower texture can help you identify it. The flowers bloom regardless of the weather conditions at any given time. This perennial plant can reach a height of more than 50 cm. Five white or pink petals and five green sepals make up the flowers.

The flower is 3 to 9 cm wide, with petals measuring the length of the sepal three times. Vervain mallow leaves have long petioles that range in length from 3 to 8 cm. The tops of the leaves are typically dark green, with lighter green underneath.

**Edible Parts**

Vervain mallow's seed, flowers, and leaves are all edible. The seeds are the most delicious part of the plant.

**Safe Consumable Quantity**

It is best to consume food in moderation.

**Best Consumable Condition**

The leaves are mild and can be eaten raw or cooked

**Nutritional  value**

The plants are high in vitamin E, vitamin C, and magnesium.

**Location**

It is a widespread plant in North America. They are typically found in wastelands or thickets.

**Cactus Prickly Pear**

The prickly pear cactus originated in South America before migrating to Mexico and the southern United States. It depicts fifteen other Opuntia species found in North America.

**Identification**

They are perennial plants distinguished by fleshy, jointed, and flattened stem segments known as the pads. Pads are modified stems or branches that serve various functions in the plant. They are also in charge of water storage, flower production, and photosynthesis.

Their flowers typically bloom from April to June. Some species can be yellow, peach, orange, cream, or any combination of these colors. They don't have any leaves. Prickly pears can reach a height of 1.5 meters and a diameter of 4.5 meters.

**Edible Parts**

Both the fruits and the pads are safe to eat. The edible prickly pears have pads that resemble a beaver's tail. The cholla cacti, which are distinguished by their slender and rounded stems, are not edible.

**Safe Consumable Quantity**

Some people may experience nausea and abdominal pain if they consume too much of it.

**Best Consumable Condition**

Its fruits can be eaten fresh.

**Nutritional value**

It contains a lot of carbohydrates, protein, vitamins A and C, calcium, and phosphorus.

**Location**

The majority of prickly pear species are native to North America.

**Robert Herb**

Herb Robert was named after a French monk who used the plant to treat a variety of diseases. It was widely known as a powerful cure for internal and external ailments in the year 1000 AD.

Scientists discovered that the plant thrives in areas with high radiation levels, according to research. According to the findings, the plant absorbs and disperses radiation from the ground.

## Identification

The plant is easily identified by its unpleasant odor and bright pink color. The flower blooms from spring to autumn. The flower is radial star-shaped and measures 1.5 to 2 cm across at its widest point. It has five petals with round tips and paler veins. The flower can have up to ten stamens, and the pistil has five carpels.

The leaves are partially dark green and measure about 6cm in length, with purple edges. Even when the plants are picked frequently, the plant is known to produce an abundance of leaves. Herb Robert can reach a height of 30 to 40 cm in their lifetime.

## Edible Parts

Both the flower and the leaves are safe to eat. They can be dried and stored for use during the winter. Mosquitoes can be repelled by rubbing fresh leaves on the skin.

## Safe Consumable Quantity

Consume as you see fit.

## Best Consumable Condition

It can be consumed raw or fresh.

## Nutritional value

It's high in vitamins A and C, as well as carotenoids.

## Location

It's common throughout most of North America.

## Mayapple

This perennial plant is a member of the Barberry family. Its distinctiveness stems from its two umbrella-like leaves, which mature into one flower. The plant is easily identified from a distance because its rhizomes form dense mats. It typically thrives in moist, humus-rich soils.

### Identification

During the spring, mayapple is one of the few plants that sprout from the ground. It is easily identified by its large, deeply cut leaves. A flower grows beneath the leaves and eventually turns into a yellow fruit.

Flowers with 6 to 9 petals emerge from the leaf axils.

Its large greenish-yellow ovary is surrounded by yellow stamens.

Mayapple leaves stand out due to their large umbrella-like leaves. The leaves remain closed as the stem grows longer, eventually unfolding to about 15 cm across. The leaves continue to grow until they reach a total length of about 40 cm across. Mayapples are typically 30-40 cm tall, with a stout and smooth stem.

**Edible Parts**

The yellow fruit is the only edible part of the mayapple. Before eating, the seed must be removed. Before eating, make sure the fruit has turned yellow because unripe fruits are unsafe to eat. The fruit can also be used to make smoothies.

**Safe Consumable Quantity**

Overeating it may result in colic. You should only consume a small amount.

**Best Consumable Condition**

Only the ripe yellow fruit is edible.

**Location**

It is common throughout North America.

Joe Pye weed is a multifunctional wild plant. It is grown as a herb, as butterfly plants, and in some places as flower beds.

People believe the plant was named after a Native American named Joe Pye (Jopi). In the nineteenth century, he used the plant to treat typhus. It is a perennial plant that blooms after other plants have finished blooming.

## Identification

The plant is distinguished by pink or purple flowers at the tip of its stem. From around July to late fall, the flowers appear on the stems. They have a large flower head with a cluster of pink disk flowers in a domed cluster. The leaves form a concentric circle and can reach a height of about 25 cm. Each node has four to seven blades and elliptical leaves. Joe Pye weed can reach a height of about 1 meter. They can be found mostly in marshes, moist woods, damp thickets, along streams, and in fields.

**Edible Parts**

Any part of the plant, including the root, can be eaten. You can save the leaves and stems for later use by drying them. Herbal tea can be made with fresh flowers.

**Safe Consumable Quantity**

It is best to consume in moderation.

**Best Consumable Condition**

It is best eaten fresh or dried and stored for later use.

**Location**

The plant originated in North America.

**Knapweed**

Knapweed's botanical name is Centaurea nigra, and it is also known as Hardheads. As a neglected grassland or grazed pasture, Knapweed can live for years. Its flowers are pollinated by insects such as flies, bees, beetles, and butterflies.

## Identification

Knapweed thrives in areas with poor to moderate soil fertility. The plant can be identified by its dull green color and rough hairs. They have upright stems that branch at the top.

The flower heads of knapweed grow at the tips of the branches, with the base covered in dark fringed margins. The flower blooms from June to September, depending on location.

The leaves are pale green and alternate. Lower leaves on the plant are toothed and can grow to be about 25 cm long. Knapweed can grow to be about 1 meter long in its lifetime. They are common in meadows, pastures, field borders, woodland edges, and roadside ditches.

## Edible Parts

Knapweed is commonly used in traditional medicine. Only the flowers are fit for human consumption.

## Safe Consumable Quantity

Consume as you see fit.

**Best Consumable Condition**

Depending on your preferences, you can eat it raw or cooked.

**Nutritional value**

It's high in carbs, protein, fiber, and ash.

**Location**

It's common in Canada and a few other parts of North America.

**Wild Leek**

Wild leeks are related to onions and are one of the first edible wild plants to appear in the spring. It was traditionally used as a spring tonic to aid in recovery after a long winter.

There are two types of wild leeks: Var. tricoccum and variants burdickii. The former has a red base and a cluster of approximately 50 flowers. The latter has narrow leaves in clusters of about 20.

**Identification**

Wild leeks have an elliptical-shaped leaf that blooms in the spring. They are easily identified by their scent, which is similar to that of onions. To tell the difference correctly through the onion scent, you may need to crush its leaf.

For about four weeks after the leaves emerge, the flowers bloom. The resulting white flower has six petals and six stamens with a creamy yellow tip.

During the early spring, the leaves sprout from an underground bulb. They can reach lengths of 15 to 30 cm and widths of 2 to 10 cm. It has a smooth texture and parallel veins. Wild leeks are mostly found in forests and grow to be about 45 cm long.

## Edible Parts

The leaves and bulbs are both edible. Because of the plant's seven-year growth cycle, it is best to take one leaf per plant.

## Safe Consumable Quantity

Consume as you see fit.

## Best Consumable Condition

The leaves and bulbs can be consumed raw or cooked.

## Nutritional value

It contains a lot of vitamins and minerals.

## Location

It can be found throughout North America.

**Cleavers**

Cleavers are members of the Rubiaceae family. The Rubiaceae family contains over 3000 species. Other names for the plant include sticky bud, sticky willy, kisses, sticky weed, and clivers.

## Identification

Cleavers are an annual plant with spreading stems that creeps. With hooked hairs, they grow by attaching themselves to anything in their path. The flowers are tiny, measuring about 1mm long and 1–2mm wide. They are white and have four petals that are joined at the base.

Cleavers produce two types of leaves: stalkless leaves and cleaver leaves. At the stem joint, the stalkless leaves grow in groups of 6 to 9.

Cleaver leaves are narrow and have pointed tips. Except when they attach themselves to a tall plant, they do not grow in height. Cleavers are frequently found along field margins and in hedgerows.

**Edible Parts**

Both the leaves and the stems are safe to eat. They were also used for medicinal purposes in the past. Fruit can be dried as well as a coffee substitute I Some people dry the leaves for tea.

**Safe Consumable Quantity**

You are free to eat whenever you want. If you get a rash after touching the plants, don't eat it.

**Best Consumable Condition**

The leaves and stem are edible both raw and cooked. It can also be used in sandwiches.

**Location**

It is found primarily in North America, Europe, and Asia.

**Cattail**

Cattails, also known as bulrushes, are among the most popular wild foods. They are commonly used to make mats and baskets. The Aboriginals used the plant to make flour.

## Identification

Cattails are distinguished by their cigar-shaped, brown heads. During the spring, the young shoots develop into a cigar-like head. This cigar contains thousands of growing seeds.

The male and female cigar-like formations make up the flowers.

The male portion is represented by the yellow spike that rises above the female portion.

Cattail leaves are erect, linear, flat, and dome-shaped, with widths ranging from 10 to 20 mm. Each vegetative shoot generates 12 to 16 leaves. Cattails are upright plants that grow to a height of 2 to 3 meters.

## Edible Parts

The plant's young stems can be eaten raw or cooked. Some people garnish the salad with the lower part of the leaves. Some people roast the blossoming flowers, and the yellow pollen is commonly used in pancakes.

After thoroughly shaking the pollens in a paper bag, they can be used as a thickener in stews and soups.

## Safe Consumable Quantity

Consume as you see fit.

## Best Consumable Condition

Choose the younger edible parts and eat them raw or cooked.

## Nutritional value

It contains a lot of carbohydrates and protein.

## Location

Swamps, open wet areas, moist fields, and ditches are ideal habitats for them.

## BlueVervain

The Verbenaceae family includes Blue Vervain. Apart from being a wild plant, it has also become one of the most popular options for

Garden landscaping It is a perennial flower that is frequently pollinated by bees.

## Identification

Blue Vervain is distinguished by its 4-angled stems, which occasionally have white hairs. It's a tall, upright plant with branches above the midpoint. Blooming occurs from late spring to late summer, depending on the geographic location.

The wildflower has numerous pencil-like tips that branch upward. Each flower has a ring of purple flowers around it. Blue Vervain leaves are opposite one another and range in length from 3cm to 17cm.

They are distinguished by their dark green color and prominent veins. Blue Vervain can reach heights of up to 2 meters in its lifetime.

**Edible Parts**

The seed, flower, and leaves are all safe to eat. Only the ground and roasted forms of the seed are edible. To garnish a salad, toss the flowers and leaves into it. Medical herbalists use it for medicinal purposes as well.

**Safe Consumable Quantity**

You can eat as much as you want of it. People suffering from kidney disease should avoid eating this plant.

**Best Consumable Condition**

The leaves and flowers are edible both raw and cooked. The seed can only be eaten after it has been ground or roasted.

**Location**

It is a common plant in the United States and Canada. It thrives in moist environments with little exposure to sunlight.

**Common Yarrow**

Achillea millefolium is another name for Common Yarrow. It is a perennial weed that is commonly referred to as a weed.

The name Achillea was derived from Achilles, who used it to heal his soldiers' wounds during the Trojan War.

**Identification**

Common Yarrow is distinguished by its aromatic and fern-like green foliage. They consist of tiny dense flowers that flatten out. It is a common plant that can be found in both the wild and in gardens. Flower heads form clusters on the stem, with each cluster containing at least one flower head. Each flower head has 20 to 25 white ray flowers.

This plant's leaves can grow to be 7 to 12 cm long. On either side of each midrib, numerous leaflets are further subdivided into smaller leaflets. Yarrow plants typically grow between 30 cm and 1 meter in height.

## Edible Parts

Both the flowers and the leaves are edible. They are suitable for making tea.

A salad with the leaves can also be a delicious combination.

## Safe Consumable Quantity

A moderate or small amount should be used each time.

## Best Consumable Condition

The leaves of this wild plant can be eaten raw or cooked, and they are best eaten when they are young.

## Location

It is a common plant that can be found throughout most of North America. They thrive in sunny conditions with sandy soil.

## Commons Soe Thistle

The Compositae family includes the common sow thistle. It is popular due to its high mineral content.

## Identification

They are easily identified by their hollow stems that eject latex when broken. The leaves are lobed and the taproot is short. The flowers are yellow and have a diameter of 5 to 6 mm. The flowers are found near the plant's branch end on the stalk.

The first set of leaves has a toothed margin and is round. The leaves have hairs on the surface, and the mature leaves are thinner. The mature leaves are dark green with a toothed border. The plant can reach a height of 30cm to 1m. The plant grows well in most soil types and can be found in yards, pastures, and fields, among other places.

## Edible Parts

This plant's flowers, leaves, and young roots are edible.

## Safe Consumable Quantity

Consume as you see fit.

## Best Consumable Condition

The plant tastes best when it is young. Flowers and leaves can be added to salads or cooked alongside spinach and soups. You can also prepare the young roots and stems.

**Nutritional value**

It contains minerals such as magnesium, calcium, potassium, sodium, iron, phosphorus, zinc, and vitamins.

**Location**

Although it is native to Europe, it can be found in many parts of North America.

**Coltsfoot**

Coltsfoot is a perennial plant that is known as the "son before the father" because the flowers appear and die before the leaves. When the plant blooms in the spring, it resembles a dandelion. Some people use it to treat and prevent coughing.

**Identification**

It can be identified by its bright yellow flowers, which bloom in early Spring. The flowers are single and about 1.5 cm wide on average. The flowers have many pistillate flowers and ray florets with white stamens.

The leaf's surface is smooth and waxy in appearance. White hairs are scattered beneath the leaves. The average height of Coltsfoot is about 10 to 15 cm.

**Edible Parts**

Both the flowers and the leaves are safe to eat. Safe Consumable Quantity

Because the leaves have a slightly bitter taste, it is best to use in moderation.

**Best Consumable Condition**

Salads can also benefit from the edible parts. Coughs can be relieved by combining the flower with honey. The leaves have a slightly bitter taste and should be boiled before adding to a soup.

**Location**

It prefers open areas and can be found along roadsides, ditches, forest edges, and landslides.

## Fern Leaf Yarrow

Achillea filipendulina is another name for Fern Leaf Yarrow. It is well-known for its antiseptic and anti-inflammatory properties.

It is high in minerals and vitamins that are good for your health. It is also used to treat colds, kidney diseases, menstrual pain, wounds, and a variety of other ailments.

### Identification

The single stout stem distinguishes this wild plant. This stem bears disk flowers and tiny rays. Yellow flowers grow in large clusters known as compound corymbs. Corymbs can grow to be up to 10 cm across.

The leaves range in length from 5 to 20 cm. On the stem, they grow almost evenly and curly.

### Edible Parts

Salads benefit from the young leaves. It is frequently used as a beer preservative.

### Safe Consumable Quantity

Although the plant is nutritious, it is not recommended that it be consumed on a regular basis.

**Best Consumable Condition**

The bitter leaves can be eaten raw or cooked.

**Location**

It is widespread in North America and many other parts of the world. They are typically found in rural areas, waste areas, along highways, meadows, and pastures.

***Last Words***

Knowing everything there is to know about a wild plant will help foragers understand what works best in each season. The majority of these wild plants are in your immediate vicinity. You can choose to incorporate some into your landscape for easy access. There is always a plant to be found, whether you are a novice or a seasoned forager.

It is not enough, however, to simply locate these plants. You must understand how to harvest and store them correctly. That will be covered in the following chapter.

# CHAPTER 7:

## *Harvesting and Stockpiling Techniques of Wild Edible Plants*

Harvesting and storing are two important aspects of foraging. Harvesting encompasses all of the processes involved in bringing profits back from the field. All processes involved in ensuring the continued use of harvested proceeds are referred to as storage.

The demand for wild edible plants has recently increased. This increase in demand is due to a greater awareness of health and wellness. Many restaurants have begun to include wild species on their menus.

It is not cheap, as are many other healthy food options. Restaurants pay a high price for these wild species. The majority of restaurants would pay a premium to have their plants delivered fresh. Unfortunately, the majority of these species are endangered. You must always ensure that your plants are delivered fresh.

Some of these species are seasonal as well. Demand, on the other hand, does not follow a seasonal pattern. Finding a way to protect them from scarcity gives you a price advantage.

As a result, harvesting and storage are inextricably linked.

Even if you keep them for personal reasons, storage is essential. Foraging can be a stressful experience. Storage allows you to keep some for later use. You won't have to go out looking for wild plants every time.

**Wild Plant Harvesting Tips**

Wild plant harvesting can be a lot of fun. It can also be disastrous, especially if you are inexperienced. The issue here is you.

You could be doing something wrong unknowingly. As a result, even if you're a seasoned harvester, the following harvesting tips will come in handy.

**1. Gather Identification Information**

This step should not be overlooked. It is critical because some plants are toxic to consume. Some of these dangerous plants are related to edible plants. Some plant families are not generally edible. While harvesting, you may come across many similar relatives.

To avoid picking potentially dangerous plants, make sure you get proper training. Before going to the field, familiarize yourself with your plants.

While some plants are poisonous when consumed, others are lethal when touched. Some species can cause severe allergic reactions simply by touching them.

Before you go to the field, you should be aware of what to avoid. More importantly, you should comprehend why you should avoid them.

## 2. Recognize the Situation

Before you go out to harvest, you should be familiar with the area. Your ideal harvest location should be pollution-free. Herbicides and insecticides are examples of pollutants. The area should also be free of hazardous waste.

Examine the plants' growth conditions as well. Plants that are struggling to grow should not be selected. Plants growing in drought or with low soil fertility, for example, should be avoided.

More importantly, only harvest in areas where it is legal.

Also, try to change the harvest location as frequently as possible.

## 3. Recognize the Plant

Understanding the plant can take many forms. You should also learn how to harvest the plants in the most effective way possible without killing them. As a result, the plants will be useful for as long as you require them.

Knowing when to harvest your plants is an important part of understanding them. When different plants are at their best, they have different seasons. Furthermore, their parts perform well at different times of the year. Do some research to determine the best time to harvest what you require.

## 4. Harvest Only What You Need

When considering seasonality, you may be tempted to take a little too much. It is incorrect on several levels.

To begin with, you may be putting the species in danger of extinction. If you continue to harvest so much, you may have harvested all of the species available for harvest.

Second, taking too much at once may result in waste. You might take so much that you can't store it. It is eventually discarded.

To avoid waste, you should have an idea of how much you need. Some species can be stored properly for up to six months. This period lasts longer than most wild species' offseason. As a result, your estimates should project how much you will require for that length of time.

Only about 5% of a species' population should be harvested. Such species should be plentiful in your harvest area.

Remember that you are not the only one harvesting. As a result, harvest in a way that leaves a lot for others.

## 5. Following Harvest

After you've harvested your plants, you should consider the future. Replace the plants with their seeds if the opportunity arises. You'd have something to fall back on in the future that way.

## Wild Plant Storage Suggestions

The following suggestions will assist you in preserving your harvest and preserving its freshness.

1. Keep your plants moist.

It is possible to pick your plants with water while collecting them. You may find dew on them, especially if you harvest early in the morning. Remove the water droplets if you want to store them for a long time.

2. Store separately

Keep different species separately. This method will keep contamination at bay.

When necessary, keep different plant parts separate from one another. For example, if you are collecting flowers and roots, keep the roots separate from the flowers. As you may know, the roots bring dirt with them, which can harm the flowers.

Green parts should be stored in paper bags instead. Containers that allow them to breathe could be used. Whatever you choose, avoid overfilling.

## 3. Refresh Prior to Storing

Try to refresh your plants as soon as you leave the field before storing them. Rinse them in cold water to restore them. This method will keep them fresh and clean for as long as you require them.

## 4. Refrigerate as soon as possible

Refrigerate your greens as soon as you get home from the field. Sort out any other parts that require refrigeration and do the same. This practice would help them keep their freshness and avoid wilting.

The distance between the harvest point and the field can be considerable at times. If possible, consider using cooling units.

## 5. Avoid the Use of Plastic

Plastic, no matter how careful you are, raises the temperature. Increased temperature will always have a negative impact on your plants' storage. Find healthy alternatives to plastics as much as possible.

*Last Words*

Harvesting and storing wild plants are critical components of foraging. The two processes frequently coexist. Both methods aim to produce plants that are safe to consume indefinitely.

Foraging requires extreme caution. We've provided some pointers to keep in mind when going foraging.

# CHAPTER 8

## *Foraging Suggestion*

Foraging can be an exciting experience, but it can also be done incorrectly. It all comes down to following the rules. Fortunately, these guidelines or rules are simple to follow. Purchasing this book is a positive step in the right direction.

The advice provided below will help you whenever you go foraging. These are some basic guidelines to follow before, during, and after you go foraging.

**Foraging Tips in General**

Before you go foraging, there are a few things you should know. We have provided these suggestions to assist you on your journey.

**Understand Your Region**

It is critical to understand the area where you will be foraging. Conduct thorough research on the landscape of the area where you plan to forage.

Emissions from mines or other industrial structures may contaminate the water or soil that feeds the plant you plan to forage. These contaminants have the potential to make you sick.

Mushrooms quickly absorb pollutants. Picking mushrooms near industrial areas or busy roads should be avoided.

Furthermore, the types of herbicides, pesticides, or other chemicals used can have an impact on the plants and, as a result, on you. As a result, make sure you do your homework.

This procedure necessitates extensive research on the terrain. Online courses and eBooks, like one, are excellent places to begin. Knowing your region allows you to learn about the plants that are grown there. This understanding leads us to the second point.

**Understand Your Plants**

Foraging includes the use of poisonous wild plants. As a result, you should be able to distinguish between edible and non-edible plants. A minor blunder can be costly. Some plants can be extremely harmful to your health.

Common wild plants in North America include giant hogweed, iris, poison hemlock, and monkshood. These plants are unfit for human consumption. So, if you're going foraging in North America, you'll need to be able to identify and avoid these plants.

- Plants such as cattails, pine, and mint are edible and safe regardless of location. Some additional tips that will help you are; Foraging with an expert - someone who can correctly identify these plants - is recommended.

- When in doubt, stick to your strengths. You can investigate the common plants you are familiar with.

- Foragers should follow the rule of thumb: if you can't identify it, don't eat it.

- It is best to progress from known edible plants to unknown edible plants. However, in extreme cases of starvation, make sure to test plants for the first time before consuming them.

**Plant Edibility Testing Tips**

- Divide the plant into different parts, such as stems and leaves, and test each separately.

- Plant parts or secretions with a bad odor or taste, such as sap, should be discarded.

- Wait ten minutes after touching your skin with a small piece of the plant. This action assists you in testing for contact poisoning.

- If you experience any type of reaction, such as rashes or inflammation, do not consume the plant. If no reaction occurs, place a small portion of the plant on your lips.

- Allow another ten minutes. Then, taste the plant with your tongue. Wait another ten minutes. If no reaction occurs, eat a small portion of the plant.

- Allow 7-10 hours to pass. If you suspect you are becoming ill, try to induce vomiting. Then avoid eating the plant.
- You're good to go if you feel good after these steps.

Remember that you should only use these tips in extreme circumstances.

The first step is to correctly identify your plants and your surroundings.

Furthermore, these tips may not be very effective for mushrooms. Some mushrooms taste delicious, but they are completely poisonous. Mushrooms must be handled with extreme caution.

You can look up a list of dangerous plants in your area and how to identify them on the internet. When foraging, books or guides make excellent companions. Books with illustrations of edible and poisonous plants are excellent sources of information.

If you're not sure, don't eat it!

**Ask Questions**

Inquire with the locals (if there are natives present). These locals are more knowledgeable about the plants than you are. You can learn more about the land and plants. They could act as a guide for your foraging expedition. Here are some pointers to consider: Plants that are suitable for animals are not necessarily suitable for humans.

Make no such assumption. Do not experiment with two new plants at the same time. After the order, try one new plant. Clean your plants thoroughly. Mushrooms must be thoroughly cleaned because they have accumulated manure, which may contain fungi or bacteria. Berries, on the other hand, must be washed with a gentle stream of water. When washing your plants, use clean water. Keep an eye on your children while foraging with your family. Allow them to eat no plants on their own. Avoid plants grown by the side of the road. If you must eat roadside plants, make sure to thoroughly wash them to avoid contamination. Some plants should not be eaten raw. When eaten fresh, some mushrooms are poisonous. Some would have to be boiled while others would have to be cooked. Look into safe ways to prepare wild plants. In addition, liver flukes in their larval stage are found in wet plants and can cause serious health problems. These issues are avoidable by cooking or boiling the plants. Different wild plants and mushrooms grow at different times of the year. To know what to expect when foraging, research plants and their seasons. Some mushrooms grow at specific times of the year. During the winter, for example, acorns, blackberries, and chestnuts are abundant.

**Understand Yourself**

You must keep a list of your food allergies and sensitivities. Avoid plants that may cause allergic reactions. It is not necessarily good for you because it is good for your friend. If you are unsure whether you are allergic to a specific plant, perform the edibility test described above. When pregnant, stay away from wild plants and mushrooms. Wild plants and mushrooms may contain noxious chemicals.

**Considerations for Foraging**

To avoid waste, do not take more than you can consume.

Take care when harvesting plants to avoid causing damage to them. Harvest with caution. Pick berries with extreme caution. Harvest from densely populated species. Take mushrooms with their caps already open. They've shed their spores in order to reproduce. Every forager should be aware of the environment. Foraging activities can sometimes cause havoc in the ecosystem. To avoid this issue, it is recommended that you begin with weeds. Some plants begin to grow almost immediately after being harvested. Plantain and nettle are two examples of weeds that grow quickly and are not harmful to humans. Don't take all of the plants. Always leave some plants behind for the sake of preservation and the ecosystem. These plants are eaten by birds and other animals. Remember that others forage as well. Some of these plants require replacement. They must produce seeds and spores in order to continue growing. It contributes to continuity and balance. Some wild plants, particularly rare plants, are protected by law. Make sure you are familiar with the plants you are permitted to forage. A field guide can also be useful when foraging. Ascertain that you have obtained permission from the landowner. The owners could be indigenous peoples or the government. You do not want to harvest plants on private or public property. Keep track of new plants, new locations, and any other information you come across. It will be your guide in the future when you go foraging. After each foraging session, clean your surroundings. Never go foraging alone in an unfamiliar area. Travel in groups, either with natives or with an expert.

**Foraging Clothing Suggestions**

Lightweight, comfortable clothing is ideal for foraging. Hiking requires a pair of jeans, a long-sleeved shirt, and comfortable running shoes or hiking boots. You'd need to protect your skin from insect bites. You can also bring insect repellent with you. Make sure you're completely covered from head to toe. If you must, wear socks. Supplies or equipment that would be useful include scissors, paper, and cloth bags, a sharp knife, and a trowel, all contained in a convenient bag pack. Make sure you don't overburden yourself with unnecessary items.

**Additional Foraging Tips for Hiking Activities**

It's not uncommon to see people combining foraging and hiking. In most cases, they complement each other. These pointers should be followed in addition to the instructions given above. These plants may not always be enough to keep you going on your journey. Your journey would necessitate a supply of healthy fats and proteins. As a result, it is critical to supplement feeding with a minimalist diet. Get some nuts or other nutritious foods. Remember, this is a low-carb diet, so don't overeat. Fish is an excellent source of protein. When foraging, you can bring your fishing equipment with you. Take your knife and go foraging. Knives aid in the harvesting of plants that must be dug up.

These tips will help you stay safe while foraging. As a result, you must forage alongside them. You may be concerned, wondering if foraging is worthwhile given all of the guidelines you must follow.

The next chapter will teach you all about the advantages of foraging. We will also assist you in assessing the risks and devising solutions to overcome them.

# CHAPTER 9

## *Environmental Advantages and Foraging's Dangers*

The personal benefits of foraging are numerous. It provides a low-cost means of obtaining one's meals. You get to handpick your food while foraging. If you're lucky, you might come across a rare species. All of these advantages are provided for free.

The number of edible plants in the wild is many times that of what we have in grocery stores. Some of these plants cannot be collected due to transportation issues.

When compared to the available supply of some species and the harvesting process, it is sometimes economically unwise to collect some species. It might not be profitable on a large scale.

Foraging, on the other hand, allows you to sample some of these species. Small amounts of these distinct flavors can sometimes be everything.

You get nourishment while treating yourself to some once-in-a-lifetime flavors. Wild species are known to be more nutrient-dense than domesticated species.

Wild dandelions, for example, have approximately seven times the phytonutrient content of spinach. Similarly, depending on the variety, wild apples may contain 100 times more phytonutrients than grocery store apples.

Furthermore, you can be certain that the food is fresh and uncontaminated. You can be assured of relative safety because you get to pick your own food.

You get to see the outside world while picking up fresh and tasty food. Hike to harvest locations and stretch your legs to pick some fruits. This type of exercise has its own set of benefits. It may even be more rewarding than going to the gym.

Some things have been taken away from us by modern society. Connecting with the environment is one of these things.

Instead of simply watching from afar, you are directly involved with nature. You can tell natural cycles and reconnect with the natural world. Simply looking at some plants can tell you what season it is. You can also predict which plants will be abundant at those times.

Is there a better way to connect with nature? Foraging allows you to connect with the environment naturally.

The benefits of foraging on the environment are the apex of it all. Without a doubt, foraging is beneficial. However, there are concerns that it will have a negative impact on the environment.

Almost everything that has an advantage also has a disadvantage. Similarly, foraging has drawbacks, even on a personal level. For example, one could consume dangerous species. It is also possible to be arrested, and so on.

In this chapter, we will look at the environmental benefits of foraging. We will also investigate the environmental consequences of foraging.

**Environmental Advantages of Foraging**

Foraging is good for the environment. Here are a few ways that foraging can benefit the environment.

1. Long-term viability

The ability of a species to exist indefinitely is referred to as its sustainability. To be sustainable, a species must be consumed reasonably. These species must be used without causing extinction.

It is critical because extinction affects more than just the species.

From a broader perspective, the consequences could be significant.

Many people believe that not eating wild plants helps to preserve the species. To put it simply, the best way to exhaust something is to consume it. Foragers, on the other hand, defend the species they consume.

This is due to the fact that foraging is done ethically. Although informal, these ethics ensure the species' survival.

Foragers, for example, must spread plant seeds after harvesting. It would allow the plants to regenerate. Furthermore, foragers are only permitted to take 5% of the total population of a plant species in place.

2. Greater Biodiversity

Foraging improves biodiversity when done correctly. Biodiversity describes the diversity of an ecosystem. That is, how many different plant and animal species live in a given environment.

According to scientists, the world contains approximately 80,000 edible plants. Approximately 95% of what we eat today comes from 30 of those plants. It leaves over 99% of the resources unutilized.

The success of the species we eat today is due to man's reliance on them for survival. As an example, consider rice. Man likes to eat rice. A lot of effort has been put into rice over the years to ensure that it does not become extinct.

Foraging increases the variety of plants on which we can rely. It provides us with more plants to protect consciously. This action implies that we will also want these plants to succeed.

Furthermore, a recent study claims that careful plant collection is beneficial to plant populations.

3. Sustainable Food Production

A lot of chemical inputs are used in regular food production. Fertilizers are applied to the soil in order to increase productivity. Herbicides Weed killers are used to kill weeds, and insecticides are used to keep insects at bay. The list goes on and on.

The cropping system that we currently have has a limited scope. This system prefers cultivated species over what it considers weeds. Finally, these weeds are doomed to extinction by any means. In most cases, hazardous chemicals are used.

Some of these chemicals are found in the plants we eat.

They accumulate in the body and cause harm over time.

On a larger scale, the use of these chemicals has negative environmental consequences. Using a chemical fertilizer, for example, may appear to be risk-free. Unfortunately, it has the potential to pollute waterways. It increases the number of greenhouse gases in the atmosphere.

Pesticides and rodenticides are lethal to wildlife. These chemicals eventually reduce biodiversity.

Foraging is a more environmentally friendly alternative to conventional agriculture. Forage plants grow naturally, eliminating the need for chemicals that may harm the environment.

In addition, foraging provides an alternative to our monotonous cropping systems. Many of the species we call weeds can be consumed through foraging.

Some of these 'weeds' are actually more nutritious than cultivated plants. It's more of a win-win situation when it comes to foraging. Consuming some of the 'weeds' nourishes you. You can also control their population so that they do not harm your crops.

Personal safety is guaranteed while foraging. You are also assured of the safety of the environment.

4. Development of New Habitats

The species that we now refer to as domesticated were once wild. They existed long before man discovered how to cultivate these species.

Man discovered how to reproduce these plants without constantly collecting them. Because of this evolution, a man had to take seedlings of these plants from the wild.

It can sometimes result in the introduction of unwanted plants. This unintentional introduction results in the formation of new, distinct ecosystems.

5. Nature Appreciation

Foraging allows people to interact with their surroundings. By doing so, they can learn to appreciate the environment and become more concerned about it.

Foraging aids in the understanding of the seasons. You are familiar with food cycles, which means that you must wait for certain seasons to enjoy certain foods. This is a different way of life than you are accustomed to. It helps you respect the environment in some ways.

Foraging, more importantly, teaches you about the environment. You will learn the best ways to harvest your plants as well as harvesting methods that promote sustainability. You will also be educated on endangered species.

You can contribute your quota to conservation and preservation this way.

**Environmental Consequences of Foraging**

The impact of foraging on the environment is a contentious issue. Scientists who support foraging believe it is nearly harmless. On the other hand, some of them believe it is dangerous.

The truth, on the other hand, lies somewhere in the middle. Foraging, despite its numerous environmental benefits, can pose just as many risks, particularly when the forager is inexperienced or deliberately disregards instructions.

The following are examples of how foraging could harm the environment.

1. Excessive harvesting

Overharvesting is one of the most serious environmental threats posed by foraging. Let's be honest. Human beings would always be human beings. There would be a strong desire to return for more.

Keeping in mind that many of these species are expensive. People would want to harvest more, at levels that the environment might not be able to recover from any time soon. Although some scientists believe that this harvesting is beneficial to the species.

Furthermore, some scientists believe that the population of wild plants cannot support everyone. If everyone started foraging, there could be a serious overharvesting problem.

Overharvesting may eventually result in extinction. Given the fragility of ecosystems, there would be repercussions. One plant may appear insignificant. However, for many other plants and animals, one plant could be everything.

Scientists who promote foraging, on the other hand, do not see it as a problem. Humans, they believe, will always find a way to ensure their survival. That is, if humans decide to eat wild varieties, they will devise a way to keep them available indefinitely.

Even so, this takes the 'natural' out of foraging. Furthermore, some species (particularly mushrooms) are uncultivable. The question is, how do such species be replaced?

2. Species Endangerment

Accidents occur on a regular basis. We all make mistakes as humans, no matter how careful we are. The severity of these errors usually varies. In foraging, even minor errors can have serious consequences.

Little mistakes, such as unknowingly stepping on a harmless plant, can have serious consequences. Finally, you can discover that those

Plants are threatened. Furthermore, even with the greatest care, the protection of these endangered species is dependent on the forager's experience.

Veterans would quickly learn what and where to avoid. Beginners, on the other hand, may struggle. Veterans may make the same mistakes when introduced to completely new environments.

Some people get carried away with the excitement of foraging. Some people go above and beyond to obtain certain species.

Some of these individuals are motivated by the exorbitant prices of these wild plants. Others are simply captivated by their taste. In either case, you can see them throwing caution to the wind in order to satisfy their cravings.

It has the effect of trampling on endangered species. Some may even destroy tree branches in order to partake in some wild fruits.

3. Natural Ecosystem Devastation

Foraging is associated with human interference with natural environments. Though some may argue that this interference is minor, even small amounts of human intervention can tip the balance of ecosystems.

This interference could be as minor as laying down footpaths. Man, no matter how small, contributes to an imbalance in these natural habitats. These minor imbalances eventually lead to the extinction of some species.

Encouraging foraging would imply introducing a large number of humans into the wild. An influx of this magnitude would undoubtedly upset the delicate balance of these habitats.

It is currently estimated that over 12 species become extinct every day. At that rate, if we all decided to forage, it would only be a matter of time before we ran out of options.

4. Toxicology

Toxicology is one of the major risks associated with foraging. There are numerous edible species available. At the same time, several species are toxic to humans.

Some of these edibles resemble their dangerous counterparts. Experience is sometimes the best way to tell them apart. Even with experience, veterans have difficulty distinguishing between some plants.

Toxic plants, if consumed, can cause poisoning. Some others can also cause severe skin irritation in allergy sufferers.

**Last Words**

There is no doubt that foraging is advantageous. There are numerous advantages for both humans and the environment as a whole. However, the benefits of foraging are contingent on prudent use. Reasonable use is also influenced by the forager, the land, and a number of other variables.

If left unchecked, foraging can become a problem. Even with the drawbacks that come with excessive use, foraging is still beneficial.

Using the proper tools is one way to avoid making foraging a problem.

The following chapter will teach you how to obtain all of the necessary tools before going foraging.

# CHAPTER 10

## *Essential Foraging Tools*

Foraging is one of the most cost-effective and health-promoting hobbies available. It's an excellent way to reconnect with nature. It's also a great way to get outside and explore.

Foraging is a way of life for some people. Having the right tools will make foraging more enjoyable, safe, and convenient for you.

**15 Essential Foraging Tools**

Having the right tools simplifies life. If you want to go foraging, some essential tools will make your foraging experience enjoyable.

These tools make foraging easier and more enjoyable. Some of them you can live without, but others you simply cannot.

1. Tree pruners

As a forager, you might not be able to live without a pruning knife. If you can only afford one tool to get started, pruners are the best option. A pruning knife can be used to cut vines and stalks.

Pruners are designed for this purpose, and their hook-shaped design allows them to slice with a single stroke. A dedicated knife is also useful in mixed terrain and for cutting close to the ground. You get to keep your survival knife safe from rust and rock strikes.

However, selecting the proper pruning knife is critical. Purchase a high-quality, sharpenable pruner. This feature ensures that you don't have to replace your pruner every time it becomes blunt.

If at all possible, buy a pruner that can be stippled or has a non-slip handle. This feature prevents it from slipping and cutting you.

Invest in a pruner that reduces strain and hand fatigue. When fully opened, the pruners should not be wider than your grasp.

Pruners are primarily used for gathering and processing foraged herbs. They can easily sever twigs, small branches, roots, and herbaceous stems.

2. Weeding Knife or Japanese Garden Knife

Hori Hori is another name for this tool. Hori Hori is a well-known garden knife from Japan. This explains why it is known as a Japanese knife. The blade is light and comfortable to use. It is also one of the most important tools for foragers. It is small and light enough to fit into your backpack.

This compact tool is used for heavy-duty work. It's a great weeding tool as well as a sturdy wildcrafting tool. It aids in the breaking up of soil and the extraction of roots from the earth. Garden knives are strong enough to pry rocks out of the ground and can cut through most clay soils. It can also be used to divide roots, cut sod, and transplant plants.

When purchasing a garden knife, choose one with a wooden handle over one with a plastic handle. Also, look for one with a lip at the base of the blade. If the knife slips, it will protect your hand.

3. Fork for Digging

A digging fork is the best tool for digging roots. The fork tines can effectively loosen soil and lift branch roots from the ground. Digging forks is less likely than a spade or shovel to damage roots.

In the garden, a digging fork can be used to loosen soil, harvest medicinal roots, and weed. Digging forks have square and sturdy tines, as opposed to hay or manure forks, which have flat and bendable tines.

4. shovel

You almost certainly already have this tool in your garden shed or garage. However, having a variety of types can be beneficial. Shovels come in various sizes.

If you do a lot of foraging, you should use a larger, easier-to-manipulate shovel. Depending on how much foraging you do, you can also stick with the compact version.

A compact shovel is primarily used in foraging to begin the process of removing/harvesting tap-rooted plants such as burdock. It's also useful for digging in hard-packed soil.

Shovels should be appropriate for the environment in which you intend to harvest. Small digging spades work well in soft soil but are not suitable for use in rocky soil environments.

5. Kitchen Shears or Scissors

You may be wondering why you require kitchen scissors when you already own a knife. If you already have a knife, you can do without kitchen scissors.

However, keep in mind that many tasks are easier to complete with scissors than with a knife. It also does not eliminate the need for a knife, as some tasks are better accomplished with one.

In essence, they are both well-suited for different purposes. Having them both as foraging tools will therefore make foraging easier for you.

Kitchen scissors can be used to collect tender-stemmed greens such as violet, chickweed, and cleavers. Using a pruning knife for this task can muck up the job because pruners are designed for thicker stems.

Scissors are also preferable to pruners when it comes to stalked plants like Japanese knotweed, burdock, and thistles.

When shopping for kitchen scissors, look for a high-quality pair that can cut through small branches.

## 6. Trowel

A trowel is a small hand tool used to dig, smooth, apply, or move small amounts of particulate or viscous material.

Depending on the type of foraging you do, you may not need a trowel.

If you want to harvest roots like burdock, groundnuts, wild carrot, and so on, you'll need a trowel. You'll need a good way to dig these roots up, and a trowel is the best tool for the job.

To reduce the weight of your backpack, carry the trowel only when it is root season.

## 7. Knife in a pocket

When you need to peel the bark of medicinal trees, cut mushrooms off wood, or cut through thick stems, a pocket knife comes in handy. Using a pocket knife lowers your risk of injuring yourself.

## 8. Handled Baskets

Baskets will reward you in a variety of ways. They are useful for collecting and drying herbs. Baskets are a must-have for mushroom collectors.

Mushrooms squish easily, so the best way to store them is to lay them flat in the bottom of a large basket. Purchase a basket with handles for added convenience.

Furthermore, wild herbs, smaller plants, and edible flowers are better kept in a basket, where they are less likely to be bruised or crushed.

9. Rucksack

A good backpack is one of the most important foraging tools. It is the most convenient way to transport your other foraging tools as well as your finds.

A good backpack should be well-padded, with comfortable straps, and the right size for your body. A lot of pouches and pockets are also beneficial for organization.

10. Breathable Bags

When harvesting, you must have a viable means of transporting the plants you find. If you transport the plants in plastic bags that do not allow for air circulation,

If there is any airflow, the vibrant green leaves may turn brown. A breathable container is the best way to transport these plants.

You should also consider small containers for berries, mushrooms, and fruits. Certain mushrooms, berries, and soft fruits are particularly delicate. They are easily crushed in a backpack or even a loaded foraging basket.

Putting them in small containers before putting them in your backpack or basket will protect your delicate harvest.

## 11. Tubtrugs or buckets

As your foraging skills improve, you'll need buckets for larger-scale harvests like wild blueberry and elderberry, as well as muddy root harvests. A little water in the bottom of the buckets will also help to keep your herbs' leaves and stems fresh during the long car ride back home.

## 12. Gloves

Foraging can be taxing on the hands. Nettles and berry brambles can prick your fingers. If you've ever felt a sting from brushing your hand against the fine hairs of nettles, you know that gloves are essential when working with plants.

Protect your hands and fingertips from pricks by wearing gloves.

Wear leather gloves to protect your hands.

## 13. Loupe or Magnifying Glass

A magnifying lens makes spying on flowers much easier.

To correctly identify some plants and mushrooms, you must look at every detail, such as minute pore size, almost invisible hairs on plant stems, or small veins in leaves. These details are difficult to see with your eyes alone. A magnifying glass is required.

## 14. The plate of Clear Glass

For spore prints, you'll need a clear glass plate. Making spore prints is essential for distinguishing edible mushrooms from poisonous mushrooms. A transparent glass plate can be used to make spore prints.

## 15. Water Bottle

Foraging can be very thirsty. You'll need a lot of water to stay hydrated. As a result, a water bottle is an indispensable foraging tool.

When purchasing water bottles for foraging, choose a large container that can hold a lot of water. You should also get one that fits properly into your backpack.

You now have a list of all the tools you'll need before going foraging. But, before you leave, you wonder if you can bring someone with you. You may not be familiar with foraging societies. You can learn more about them in the following chapter.

# CHAPTER 11

## *Foraging Societies: What You Should Know*

Did you ever play this game as a kid where you were lost in the wilderness and had to find food for yourself? You'd probably eat the fruits of your garden, pretend to live in a wooden house, and hunt animals.

What you probably didn't realize at the time was that it was a way of life for some people. These individuals are foragers. Yes, people still live in this manner.

You may be wondering how this lifestyle can be sustained in the twenty-first century. You should be able to see why people might want to live this way based on what you've learned in previous chapters about the benefits of foraging.

However, you may be unaware of how a foraging society is structured, the culture of these people known as hunters-gatherers, and the various types of communities. This chapter will teach you everything you need to know.

**General Characteristics of Foraging Societies**

Foraging societies are made up of people who do not have a consistent source of food. Hunter-gatherers are people who hunt and gather food.

These people lead a nomadic existence, moving from location to location in search of food. They are also usually in small groups to ensure that everyone gets enough food.

Anthropologists have spent time researching these societies. Because of the various climates in which they live, foraging societies are difficult to consider as a whole. The available resources

The resources available to communities differ as well, resulting in an unavoidable variation in culture.

Some characteristics, however, are shared by all foraging societies.

We've covered a few of them below.

• Small Towns and Cities

Foraging societies are typically small in size. They also live in remote areas with few people. According to anthropologists, this trait is most likely present to ensure that the available food can sustain everyone. If they continue to live in a densely populated area, feeding may become a survival struggle.

• Nomadic Way of Life

Hunter-gatherers are typically nomadic. Though not true of all foraging societies, it is common. They only construct temporary shelters and relocate to other areas when more food and water are required. They follow the seasons, the herds, and the available resources. The Ngatatjara people of Australia are an example of such a society.

• Homemade Tools

Foragers fashion their tools from materials found in the surrounding area. However, as their development and contact with other communities has increased, they have begun to use machine-made tools.

• Resources Used Temporarily

Foraging societies always use available resources in a way that allows them to regenerate. For example, they would not uproot fruit-bearing trees, but rather collect the fruits and leave the tree to fruit again the following year. When the resources in an area reach a certain level, the foragers relocate to another area and return the following season.

• Labor Division

Everyone works in foraging societies, regardless of gender. Gender and age are usually used to divide the work. King San's

The women of the Kalahari Desert gathered food, which included fruits, melons, berries, and nuts. Simultaneously, the men performed rituals and entertained the crowd. In some other societies, men hunted and women gathered vegetation.

• Absence of Structure

Unlike Western societies, which have well-structured political and economic systems, foraging societies lack such structures. These people are frequently related, and food is frequently shared. They also do not own property, which may result in a hierarchy. This lack of a system works because the groups are usually small and related, and they don't stay in one place.

Foraging societies have a simple and consistent way of life. The major distinction is in the resources available to them. This factor, however, can still be used to classify foraging societies. The types of foraging groups are listed below.

Different Kinds of Foraging Societies

Some characteristics can be found in any foraging society. However, there are some characteristics that can be used to categorize these societies. Among the various foraging societies are:

• Societies for Pedestrians

These societies gather food by walking around. The Kung San, also known as Zhuloasi, is a well-known foraging society that falls into this category. This group has access to over 150 plant species and 100 animal species.

Zhoulasi, on the other hand, does not consume all plants. Their favorite protein-rich food is the mongongo nut. They leave the area when the resources run out or when the seasons change. In the rainy season, they live in groups of two or three families, but when it is dry and there is water, they camp out in their twenties or forties.

• Societies of Aquatic Life

These foraging societies rely on water to obtain resources and food. The Haida, also known as the Ou Haadas, are a group of people who live on Prince of Wales Island and the Queen Charlotte Islands in British Columbia.

This tribe obtains a variety of foods from the water around their homes. Scallops, halibut, otters, salmon, sea lions, and seaweed make up their diet. However, they eat more than just what they get from the water.

They also hunt land mammals such as deer and collect wild plants such as berries.

• Equestrian Organizations

This type of forager is less common than the other two. They only identify with the South American pampas and steppes, as well as the

North American Great Plains. These foragers emerged after European settlers reintroduced horses to Americans.

Aonikenks is an example of a foraging society. This society, known as the People of the South or Tehuelche, lives on South America's Patagonian Steppes. They eat roots, rhea, and seeds and hunt guanaco.

Why are Foraging Societies becoming less common?

For over a million years, foraging societies were the norm. However, it is no longer a prevalent way of life. You may be wondering why this is the case.

The Neolithic Revolution was the catalyst for change.

Agriculture began around 12,000 years ago, with the Neolithic Revolution. People had to build houses in order to stay in one place and tend to their farms. While hunters and gatherers existed until the modern era, the lifestyle has dwindled to the point where it appears to be extinct.

One of the reasons this way of life is uncommon is due to the risks involved. There is the possibility of going days without eating, as well as health risks.

Because of the benefits of foraging, many people are considering incorporating it into their current lifestyle.

If you've read this far, you're probably thinking about doing some foraging yourself. We congratulate you on taking that step and hope we were able to assist you on your journey.

# CONCLUSION

Do you recall Bob? Yes, that man who could survive in the wilderness.

When you read his story in the introduction, you probably thought what he did was impossible.

However, now that you've reached the end of this book, we hope you're convinced otherwise. You have everything you need to go foraging, and with the help of this book, you won't make a mistake.

Every word in this book has taught you how to identify and locate edible wild plants and mushrooms in your area.

Are you attempting to refresh the knowledge you currently possess? Let's talk about what you learned from this book. You now understand what foraging is, its classifications, and frequently asked questions. There is most likely no foraging issue that you cannot address right now.

Mushrooms are a fascinating species. You now understand their history and the distinction between edible and non-edible varieties. Every detail necessary for identifying, locating, and cultivating edible species has been highlighted in an easy-to-read format.

We realized that gathering these edible mushrooms was only the beginning of our journey. As a result, you learned about all of the methods for harvesting and storing mushrooms. These suggestions will allow you to savor the sweet delicacy of mushrooms for a long time.

As delicious as mushrooms can be, they can get boring if they are always a part of your meal with no variety. As a result, you must understand how to use, identify, and locate other edible wild plants.

This should not be a problem with fifty edible wild plants described and explained in this book. You should also be aware of the proper methods for harvesting and soring these plants.

Foraging has both risks and benefits. This book has outlined them for you so you know exactly what you're doing before you begin. We didn't leave you without hope, though, because we discussed safety tips that will help you when you're out in the wilderness.

The tools you need for foraging are one of the most important things to get right, especially if you are a beginner. You now understand the fifteen essential tools you must have when going foraging.

Expert foragers will almost certainly tell you that one of the joys of foraging is the opportunity to do so with friends and family. You now understand the characteristics and types of foraging societies.

Can you see that you have everything you need to begin foraging? With this book as your guide, you'd have no trouble identifying, locating, and preserving edible wild plants and mushrooms in your area.

So, what are you holding out for?

It's time to go foraging!